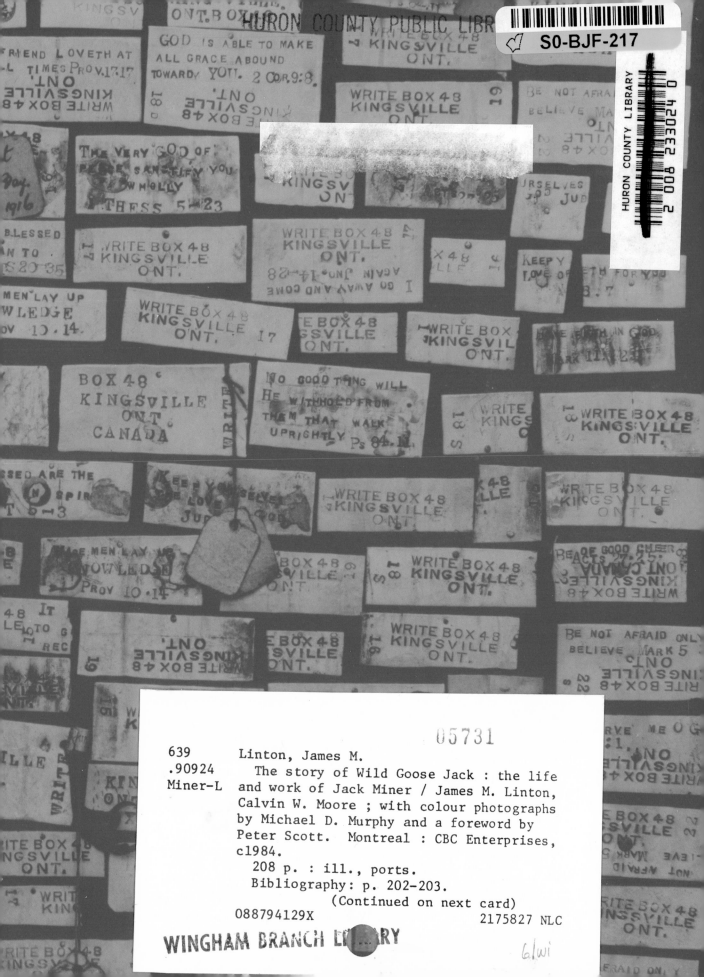

THE STORY OF WILD GOOSE JACK

JAMES M. LINTON
CALVIN W. MOORE

THE STORY OF
Wild Goose Jack

THE LIFE AND WORK
OF JACK MINER

With colour photographs by
MICHAEL D. MURPHY

and a foreword by
SIR PETER SCOTT
Chairman of Council,
World Wildlife Fund International

CBC Enterprises/Les Entreprises Radio-Canada
Montréal · Toronto · New York · London

Published by CBC Enterprises/Les Entreprises Radio-Canada, a division of the Canadian Broadcasting Corporation, P.O. Box 500, Station A, Toronto, Canada M5W 1E6.

Publié par CBC Enterprises/Les Entreprises Radio-Canada, une division de la Société Radio-Canada, C.P. 500, Succursale «A», Toronto, Canada, M5W 1E6.

The photographs by Dr. R.D. Sloane are in the Miner Collection in Kingsville, Ontario.

For further information on the film, *Wild Goose Jack* or on Jack Miner himself, write to Clear Horizon Films, Inc., 2 College Street, Suite 108, Toronto (Ontario), Canada M5G 1K3.

Canadian Cataloguing in Publication Data

Linton, James M., 1946-
    The story of Wild Goose Jack: the life and work of
Jack Miner

Bibliography: p.
Includes index.
ISBN 0-88794-129-X

1. Miner, Jack, 1865-1944. 2. Conservationists—Canada
—Biography. I. Moore, Calvin W. (Calvin William), 1951-
II. CBC Enterprises. III. Title.

QH31.M5L56 1984   639.9'092'4   C84-098235-6

General Manager/Directeur général: Guy R. Mazzeo
Publisher/Éditeur: Glenn Edward Witmer
Editor/Révision: Betty Corson
Managing Editor/Direction de la rédaction: Robert Daley
Designer/Conception graphique: Michael Solomon
Typesetter/Composition: Q Composition Inc.
Printer/Impression: Ashton-Potter Limited

Printed and bound in Canada

1 2 3 4 5 6 7 / 90 89 88 87 86 85 84

Foreword

The life of Jack Miner and his sanctuary for migratory water fowl is one of the world's most inspiring stories of man and nature. From humble origins and illiteracy, Jack Miner rose to become an outstanding champion of conservation issues and a leader in the raising of public awareness of wildlife conservation. One of his most brilliant inventions was the inscribing of Bible verses on the bands he placed on the Canada geese. When native hunters in the far north recovered these bands, not only did they receive the evangelical message; they also gained a new respect for the Canada geese.

Jack Miner was more than just a public figure; he was a sincere and honest man who applied hard work, common sense, and a deep love of nature and humanity to his everyday life. His home, the Jack Miner Migratory Bird Sanctuary in Kingsville, Ontario, has long been a mecca for tourists and nature lovers alike. Many people, including myself, have enjoyed the hospitality and warmth of the Miner family over the years, and this book is as much a tribute to Jack's sons, Manly and Jasper, as it is to their father. Year after year the Miner brothers have kept faith with their father's vision, and through their efforts his sanctuary will endure to provide a safe refuge for migrating water fowl and a thrilling spectacle for the thousands of visitors who arrive every spring and autumn.

There are valuable lessons to be learned from the story of Jack Miner. I am sure that those of you who take the time to read this book will find, as I have, many discoveries to enrich your lives.

Peter Scott.

February 6, 1984

Contents

Colour plates follow page 95.

Note to the Reader

The opportunity to create this book on Jack Miner arose from the success and interest generated by the one-hour documentary film on Jack's life entitled *Wild Goose Jack*, a production of Clear Horizon Films, Inc. The book culminates over three years of research, development, and production that my partners Jim Linton and Cal Moore and I put into the making of the film and the rediscovery of this fascinating story. *Wild Goose Jack* has won several international awards and distinctions and was first seen on television over the CBC network in April of 1983.

Many talented people contributed to the making of the film and they share with us in the success of the project. Of particular importance to us was the help we received from three specific groups. First, there are our families to thank for the encouragement and moral support they gave us throughout our work. Second, there are the individuals who put their money behind us and financed the production through the purchase of units in the film. Finally, we would like to acknowledge the National Film Board of Canada who, through its Ontario Regional Production Centre, provided the film with expert technical services and facilities without which we could not have proceeded.

It was both an honour and a privilege for our Company to be entrusted with the production of the film and this book by the Miner family. The work has been a tremendously rewarding and moving experience for all of us. On behalf of our Company I truly hope you enjoy *The Story of Wild Goose Jack*.

Michael S. Murphy

President, Clear Horizon Films
Director, *Wild Goose Jack*

11

Preface

Our first professional involvement with Jack Miner's surviving sons, Manly and Jasper, occurred in the spring of 1977. A local cable TV group for which Cal Moore then worked had undertaken a production about Jack to coincide with the unveiling of a statue of him in front of the city hall building in his home town of Kingsville, Ontario. In order to enliven the usual ceremonial footage, speeches, and interviews, Cal and his colleagues recorded Jasper and Manly's ongoing activities at the Jack Miner Migratory Bird Sanctuary, and asked the brothers if they had any old films of their father to add a period flavour to the production. Manly Miner, with the help of the official custodian of the Miner collection, Mrs. Beth Shaughnessy, located a box of 16 mm motion pictures that dealt with various periods in the sanctuary's history.

Among these rolls of film was one short reel of 35 mm which because of its format could not be incorporated into the cable TV production. But Cal noticed written on the film the words: "Mr. Flaherty. Test Roll." Robert J. Flaherty is, of course, one of the legendary figures in the history of the documentary film, and Cal immediately recognized the potential importance of this find. He contacted Jim Linton, who had been his professor in documentary film at the University of Windsor, and turned the film over to him.

Jim researched Flaherty's career but found no reference to any project on Jack Miner. He queried knowledgeable officials at the Canadian Film, Television and Sound Archives in Ottawa (where the Flaherty and other Miner films were eventually deposited), and combined this investigation with other research he conducted that summer at the British Film Institute in London and the film section of the Museum of Modern Art in New York City. The footage was even screened for the leading Flaherty experts at the latter institution, and while they acknowledged that it seemed stylistically consistent with Flaherty's work, they contended that they would need other corroborating information before forming a definitive opinion.

When Jim related these reactions to Manly Miner, Manly was greatly indignant and quickly located Flaherty's signature in the sanctuary's Registry of Visitors for the date of October 11, 1941. He then proceeded to tell the story of the genesis of the project: Jack Miner had been approached by Gabriel Pascal (the producer of the film versions of George Bernard Shaw's plays). Pascal wanted Miner to act as a technical advisor for filming scenes of birds in the production he was developing to bring Paul Gallico's *The Snow Goose* to the screen. In the process of negotiations for Jack's services, Manly apparently suggested a motion picture be made about his father, and

Pascal eventually agreed. Flaherty was enlisted as an associate producer and director, and was sent out to shoot test footage for the film. Subsequently, the project fell through and all that was ever produced was this 200-foot 35 mm test roll that Manly held onto despite Flaherty's recommendation to destroy it.

Jim asked to see any information that Manly had retained about the aborted project, but it was not until the summer of 1978 that any was found. And with the papers came an equally exciting discovery. Assisted by Mrs. Shaughnessy, Manly had located a stack of film cans in an old unheated shed on the Sanctuary grounds. They contained thousands of feet of 35 mm safety positive and nitrate negative stock (almost all of which was in good condition despite the adverse storage conditions) that had been shot by Henry Ford's cameraman between 1915 and 1940 for use by Jack on his lecture tours. As 16 mm copies were returned by the Archives for viewing and identification purposes, it became apparent that here was the nucleus for a significant film on Jack, especially since a major production dealing with him had never been undertaken.

By the fall of 1978 Mike Murphy (the eventual director of the film) had been drawn into the project, and a concerted effort to produce a film based on Jack's life had begun. After initial efforts to finance the film through government grants fell through, Clear Horizon Films was incorporated to seek private investment that could take advantage of government incentive programs for the Canadian film industry. Once the rights to the story of Jack's life and to the materials in the Miner collection had been secured from the Jack Miner Migratory Bird Foundation in the early fall of 1980, the stage was set for the actual production activities.

Rather early on in the process it became clear to Mike Murphy and us that our problem would be the opposite of that faced by many producers of historical documentaries: We generally had much more material than we could ever use in the finished film, and there were very few areas for which we lacked appropriate audio-visual resources.Clearly, much selectivity had to be exercised from the very beginning. Some things would be filmed, while others wouldn't. The process of editing the film down to a manageable length created many more difficult decisions and choices. To meet the requirements of the filmic medium, Jack's story had to be significantly shortened and simplified. As we looked at the material that lay on the cutting-room floor and that which never made it in front of the camera at all, the three of us realized that some attempt should be made to get a fuller version of Jack's story before the public. This book is in many ways, then, a product of our collective frustration with the storytelling limitations of the film medium.

There was more than that involved in the decision by the

two of us to undertake the book, however. During our years of contact and involvement with Manly and Jasper, we had grown to respect and admire their and their father's single-minded dedication to the ideal of wildlife conservation. Having steeped ourselves in material by and about Jack Miner for several years, we had come to feel we knew Jack personally, although he had died before either of us had been born. And as he had done so many times with others when he was alive, Uncle Jack was able to sensitize us to the needs for a greater awareness and practice of sound conservation activities.

The Story of Wild Goose Jack, then, is largely motivated by our concern for a rational approach to conservation in a world riddled by pesticides, acid rain, overpopulation, dramatic alterations in climatic conditions, rampant destruction of wildlife habitat—and the spectre of that ultimate horror, nuclear disaster. Despite the efforts of many concerned and dedicated individuals and groups, the degradation of the environment continues. In some ways the attitudes and approaches of those in power seem to be regressing rather than progressing, possibly as a result of an increased emphasis on jobs and the exploitation of resources that characterizes a troubled economic order.

In such a context, the ideas and activities of Jack Miner have considerable relevance. His sanctuary stands as a legacy of his lifework, and thousands of people still visit it each year. The man himself is a shining example of someone who turned personal tragedy toward social betterment, and faced adversity and opposition with dedication, good will, and a homey sense of humour. Through his crusade for conservation, he was able to convert millions to the cause of protecting God's creatures. While *The Story of Wild Goose Jack* lacks the thoroughness and detail of a full-fledged biography, it presents enough insights into the man and the impact he had on the people of the time to convey some sense of the magic that Jack worked to make conservation a living reality.

A project of this magnitude requires a great deal of support and assistance. We must thank first of all the Directors of the Jack Miner Migratory Bird Foundation, Inc. (Manly and Jasper Miner and Robert Kennedy), for allowing us to use the resources of the Miner collection as the basis for this book. Mike Murphy provided the impetus that got the book rolling in the early stages of development. Through her tireless efforts, Mrs. Beth Shaughnessy put many of the materials in the Miner collection in a form that greatly facilitated our research and writing. Lee Crawford helped us to clarify our ideas during the formative stages of the book outline, and contributed immensely to our confidence in writing the book itself by insisting that we didn't need her assistance at all.

Betty Corson demonstrated a great deal of sensitivity to the topic and much patience with us during the editing of the

15

manuscript, while Michael Solomon exhibited a sympathetic aesthetic sensibility toward the project in his role as art director. Bob Daley managed to keep the project on track with a calmness and affability that earned our admiration, and Glenn Witmer is to be congratulated for recognizing a good prospect from the outset, and encouraging the development of it.

Ann Gallant, Jean Franklin, and Sheila LaBelle all had a hand in typing the manuscript, and their valiant efforts to decipher our handwriting and meet our impossible deadline demands are greatly appreciated. Stan and Elsie Thompson frequently provided an idyllic environment for writing and their boundless hospitality did much to facilitate completion of the manuscript. Numerous individuals, many of whose words never made it to the final manuscript, kindly consented to be interviewed for both the film and the book, and their observations about Jack provided the kind of personal insights that could be obtained in no other way.

And finally, there are Shirley, Aaron, and Melissa, and Kim, who understood when the demands of writing diverted our attention from them, and who were there with encouragement when we needed it.

Jim Linton

Cal Moore

Windsor, Ontario
November, 1983

THE STORY OF WILD GOOSE JACK

Remember that it is the human race that is wild, not the birds. Birds are wild because they have to be, and we are wild because we prefer to be.

1

Taming Man's Instincts

THE figures bundled up in parkas scurry over the side of the ship and quickly make their way across the ice to where the newborn harp seals lie. As the white-coated creatures with the dark, doleful eyes look up at them, the men ready for the attack. But instead of brandishing clubs with which to crack the skulls of the seals before skinning them, these invaders are armed with cans of spray paint. Emptying the bright green contents of the cans onto the helpless pups, the men have permanently marked the prized white coats, making the pelts worthless and saving the young pups' lives in the process. Just as quickly, the "seal painters" are surrounded and arrested by a group of government officials who have been monitoring the Greenpeace members' movements since their ship left port to meet the herd before the sealers began their work. All duly recorded by the television crews and journalists who follow in Greenpeace's wake, the annual drama on the ice off Newfoundland is over for another year.

This scene and many similar to it have become an increasingly common phenomenon in the last quarter of the twentieth century. Greenpeace is perhaps the most visible group because of its wide range of concerns and its sensational approach to bringing environmental issues to the attention of the public: climbing factory smokestacks in three U.S. states to protest acid rain; chaining themselves to chairs in the Canadian Consulate in Seattle to bring attention to the seal hunt; clandestinely releasing one of two Beluga whales used in military torpedo-recovery tests off Vancouver Island to combat the use of sea mammals for military purposes; using motor-equipped rubber dinghies to disrupt oil tests by the U.S. supertanker, *B. T. San Diego*, in the Strait of Juan de Fuca to draw attention to the threat of oil exploration to coastal waters. But during this period hundreds of other groups have emerged to champion various environmental and conservation causes. Friends of Animals, Inc., Friends of the Earth, Pollution Probe, Fund for Animals, and many others have sprung up in the recent past to work with, and at times in opposition to, the older, more established nature groups such as the Sierra Club, the Audubon

A helpless harp seal pup awaits the arrival of the seal "fishermen" on the ice of the Gulf of St. Lawrence, Canada. (Barrett & MacKay/Masterfile)

Overleaf: An artist's conception of the systematic slaughter of buffalo by the early settlers of the American West, in this instance "on the Kansas Pacific." (Leslie's, June 3, 1871. Print from the Denver Public Library, Western Collection)

Society, the Boone and Crockett Club, and the Canadian Wildlife Federation. These groups have espoused a wide variety of issues all the way from saving the snail darter (an obscure, tiny fish) to the elimination of pesticides that degrade the environment, and the necessity of nuclear disarmament to remove the most potent threat to all living things.

The emergence and growth of such a large number of deeply committed environmental groups could possibly be seen as a barometer of a general growth in public consciousness about environmental and conservation matters in the modern world. On the other hand, there is a distinct possibility that people constantly bombarded by media accounts of the exploits of environmental activists become jaded about and indifferent to such problems. Public opinion surveys of the North American population have failed to reveal much general concern about "quality of life" issues. Furthermore the magnitude of the problem, as measured by the frequency and variety of media reports, may also make people feel that they are powerless to do anything about it.

It is also quite possible that the public lacks sympathy for some of the causes due to its perception of the proponents as militant, strident, and negative in their approach. Former United States Nature Conservancy chairman, Alexander B. Adams, for example, reports an incident in which he happened to mention he was a conservationist to a fellow visitor at Point Sublime in the Grand Canyon. He was taken aback by the man's show of temper and his demand to know if Adams was a member of the "Sahara Club"—a reaction reflecting a deep antipathy toward all conservationists for what he perceived to be their extremism. In some quarters this new breed of conservationists has been labelled "ultraprotectionists," "eco-activists," and "eco-freaks"—none of which would be construed as a compliment coming from the general population of mainstream North America. Such attitudes would certainly be reinforced by the incidents of infighting that seem to occur occasionally among the new groups, as well as the disagreements that often emerge between them and the more established conservation/wildlife organizations.

This modern indifference and opposition to the issue of environmental protection is mild in comparison with earlier versions of similar attitudes. The concept of "conservation" itself is a relatively modern one. The application of the word to the interrelationships among, and temperate utilization of, all natural resources is generally considered to have first been used by Gifford Pinchot in 1907. Active in forest administration and natural resource matters during Theodore Roosevelt's presidency, Pinchot advocated the prudent, nonwasteful use and renewal of natural resources, as opposed to the complete non-use concept suggested by the words "protection" and "preservation." Pinchot was only one of a growing number of people at the turn of the century who recognized that the

A man poses with massive piles of buffalo skulls and horns at the railroad siding at Saskatoon, Saskatchewan, in August, 1890. (Hugh Lumsden, C.E. Glenbow Museum, NA-354-29)

resources of North America were not a limitless bounty that could exist in perpetuity without action being taken to guard against abuses and ensure a future supply.

Examples of such enlightened conservationists were few and far between before the 1880s. The earliest of them came from among the ranks of wealthy sports hunters who had both the money and the time to allow them to worry about the protection and preservation of game, unlike market hunters who felt the need to kill as much as they could simply to provide themselves with the necessities of life—and a little extra if they were lucky. Such market hunters were merely extreme examples of the contemporary "pioneer mentality" that pictured North America as an ever-expanding frontier that would always supply enough birds and animals to meet everyone's needs.

Even the aboriginal native populations of North America were wasteful in their early hunting practices. Before they made advances in their hunting technology and skills, Indians were known to drive entire herds of animals off cliffs or surround them by fires when only a few of the herd would have supplied all their food, clothing, and other needs. With the adoption of the horse and the development of more sophisticated hunting tools, Indians were soon utilizing the more careful, efficient hunting practices with which most people now associate them. But not so the white man who invaded the Indians' homeland.

Much of the destruction of wildlife in North America was the result of the spread of population that disturbed, and in some cases destroyed, the birds' and animals' habitats. This effect was intensified by agricultural practices that involved extensive land clearing. But blood lust and the thirst for profit, abetted by the pioneer mentality, led Americans to shoot the plains bison, or American buffalo, until its vast herds were reduced to numbers that today would place it on the list of endangered species. It has been demonstrated that the army could have stopped the slaughter, but wished to see the buffalo eliminated in order to make the Indians who followed them easier to control. However, the notion that nature must be dominated and subdued, which characterized the era, and the lack of environmental foresight that such an approach engendered, were the real culprits.

These factors also determined the fate of the passenger pigeon. In the early 1800s John James Audubon and others observed flocks of the birds estimated to be over two billion in number in isolated areas alone. Perhaps because of such unbelievable numbers, the birds were harvested by the millions each year until the 1880s, when they ceased to be a viable species. But the disappearance of the passenger pigeon and the near-destruction of the bison herds were not completely in vain since they became rallying points for the earliest conservationists.

Some people speculate that the modern, intensified environmental consciousness of the new conservationists is an outgrowth of the social concern and turmoil that characterized the 1960s. Others attribute it to space satellites that sent us back photographs of the earth engulfed by swirling clouds, solidifying the notion of "spaceship earth" as a closed ecological system and banishing forever the pioneer mentality as far as our resources are concerned. American conservation historian James B. Trefethen is more specific. He credits Rachel Carson's *Silent Spring*, an account of the damage done by chemical pesticides, with being one of the most important factors in awakening Americans to the critical needs of their environment.

Although all of these are probably contributing factors, the causation is obviously too complex to be accounted for solely by these or any similarly limited explanations. Nevertheless, as mankind moves toward the end of the twentieth century, evidence is all around us that increases in population, advances in technology, and wasteful agricultural and resource practices have combined to put tremendous pressures on the world's dwindling animal, plant, and mineral "raw materials." This relentless growth and economic exploitation of our natural resources contribute to the continuing degradation of the environment of all parts of the planet, but are especially threatening to the world's remaining wilderness areas, nature preserves, and recreational parks. And as those trends intensify, increasing numbers of animals, birds, and plants are pushed to the brink of extinction. The process may be less bloody and dramatic than the elimination of the passenger pigeon, but the end result will be the same nonetheless.

We really have no idea how many animal species disappeared before the seventeenth century since there was no comprehensive system of zoological classification on which to base reliable records until the early 1600s. Estimates put the number of animals that have disappeared since 1600 at 270, consisting of 120 forms of mammals and 150 birds. Such numbers include the well-known examples of the dodo in Mauritius, the passenger pigeon in the eastern United States, and Stellar's sea cow in the arctic waters of the Bering Sea. But they also represent the relatively unknown cases of the Carolina parakeet (the only native American parrot) in Carolina, Virginia, and Louisiana; the pig-footed bandicoot (a small, vegetarian marsupial) in South Australia; and the tarpan (a plateau-dwelling pony) in Eastern Europe and Western Asia. (See the Appendix for a more complete listing of extinct species.)

Perhaps even more distressing than the over-all numbers and the specific examples, however, is the pattern of disappearance that has emerged during approximately the last 400 years. In the case of birds, for example, ten species and subspecies died out before 1700, approximately twenty in the next century, an additional twenty from 1800 to 1850, about fifty between then and 1900, and another fifty by 1970. The accelerating rate of disappearance is most marked: For birds alone, almost one form a year has disappeared over the last century, and the same figure has been quoted for mammals in recent years. Moreover, in 1972 the World Wildlife Fund reported that a total of more than 900 animals and 20,000 plants were in danger of extinction. In 1983, in Canada alone, a total of fifty-four species of birds, plants, and mammals were either extinct in Canada but existing elsewhere (extirpated), faced with immediate extinction (endangered), likely to become endangered if conditions affecting their vulnerability were not reduced (threatened), or existed in low numbers or in very restricted areas of the country (rare).

Such figures give credence to the claims that most of the great exotic wild jungle animals will be gone from their natural habitat and exist only in zoos and wildlife preserves by the end of the twentieth century. The mountain gorilla of the Uganda–Congo area of central Africa, for example, is threatened by farmers who destroy its mountain forest habitat to create improved cattle-raising areas. Similarly, the numbers of the gentle orangutan of Southeast Asia have been dropping rapidly due to their move from lowland forests to mountain regions as a result of intensified timbering operations, and due to the illicit trade in young apes that are easily captured, given their slow-moving, clumsy, and docile natures. And the finest of the four races of Asiatic elephant, the Ceylon elephant, has been killed legally in large numbers because it is capable of ruining vast areas of crops, especially its favoured sugar cane. If all of these trends continue, then it is possible for one to accept the contention that by the year 2000 as many as one million plant and animal species will be extinct—15 to 20 percent of all species on earth.

But what allows us to permit such destruction? Noted wildlife biologist Douglas Pimlott feels that it is the result of an orientation conditioned by a "subconscious pioneerism" we still harbour and a "progress ethic" that makes no sacrifice too great for development. The loss of a species is rationalized by the invocation of the natural selection mechanism of the process of evolution. Wildlife protectionist authors Noel Simon and Paul Géroudet point out, however, that while such natural selection is essentially positive when extended over long periods of geological time because it contributes to the replenishment and enrichment of life, species extinction by man "is the very antithesis of evolutionary progress, as it is characterized by biological impoverishment." Ultimately it leads to the development of what Trefethen calls "monocultures": the suppression of variety and the production of single species.

Naturalist Fred Bodsworth argues that the issue involved in conservation is not simply a matter of the amount of wilderness or wildlife that exists but also of the variety. Conservationists are not opposed to resource development *per se*, Bodsworth contends, but they do believe that if "man's heritage includes not only the works of man but also the works of creation, we have an obligation to the future to ensure that good samples of creation's multiformity of natural patterns are preserved." In addition to this moral responsibility to retain choices for future generations, others have observed that nature and wildlife conservation is motivated by the experience of aesthetic pleasure that ensues from observing and partaking of the natural world.

Most fundamentally, however, conservationists argue that protection of the natural world is in mankind's own self-interest. Ecologist J. Bruce Falls notes four such considerations: It is already known that the elimination of a species in a habitat can affect other creatures (such as the classic example of the Kaibab mule deer in the Grand Canyon National Game Preserve that, in the face of wolf, coyote, and puma elimination by farmers, increased in such numbers that they overbrowsed the vegetation, became weakened and diseased, and died in large numbers along with the protected bison and bighorn sheep that shared their food source). Nevertheless, the removal of unique species may adversely affect ecological systems in ways yet unknown; the study of such systems can help us to regulate intelligently environments altered by man in order to maintain their productivity and stability; the intellectual value of studying the natural world and the adventure in preserving fragile and non-adaptive species is bound to benefit society; and nature preserves can provide the public with an historical and ecological, as well as an aesthetic, education. Simon and Géroudet are more direct in their assessment of the importance of man's attitude and approach to nature: It is an indicator of "his capacity for dealing with fundamental issues affecting his own wellbeing and survival." Man must use his unique rational powers to see beyond his immediate short-term interests to the long-run disaster that awaits mankind if "ecological anarchy" is allowed to continue.

Environmental studies professor and naturalist film producer John Livingston sees the prescription for the saving of nature and wildlife in very different terms—if indeed such an accomplishment is possible at all. In *The Fallacy of Wildlife Conservation*, Livingston judges attempts at wildlife preservation to have been "a catastrophic, heart-breaking disaster." And the failure has not been a result of a lack of effort at presenting a rational argument: "I feel that the conventional arguments for conservation are unequal to the task, not because they are not rational (most of them try to be), but because *there is no rational argument for wildlife preservation*." Rather, the necessity for man to live in harmony with nature can only arise from the spiritual bond that the conservationist experiences with the natural world. Similar to mysticism, this "spiritual state of being that is wildlife preservation" is so vividly private and individual an experience and so resistant to classification and communication, Livingston contends, that it cannot be "reduced" and "packaged" in a form that allows it to be communicated and shared with others. It is "non-argument, non-rationality, non-sense." But in the history of the conservation movement there was one man who was able to transcend this barrier to communication, to share his spiritual bond with the natural world with others, and to use his experiences with nature to inspire others to enter the realm of wildlife conservation. That man was Jack Miner. For taming the wild Canada goose he was known as "Wild Goose Jack"; for communicating his vision and inspiring others to join his cause, he was known as "the Father of Conservation."

Jack Miner was an avid hunter before he became a conservationist, a background he shared with most of the members of the conservation movement at the turn of the century. But unlike most sports hunters who joined the struggle for game protection, Jack had been a market hunter before he discovered the camaraderie and fair play of true sports hunting. Many years afterward in his memoirs he recalled how as teenagers he and his brother Ted had used their knowledge of bird and animal habits and shooting tricks to kill as much game as possible: ". . . very few birds escaped our aim. Whether in thicket or clearing, they all brought the same price. Yes, the price was our chief motive, as we needed the money to buy warm clothing. And, since 'practice makes perfect' we two boys became expert shots and left a bloody trail behind us . . ." His admission that such practices were not sport but rather "murder in the first degree" only serves to underscore the range

Jack Miner, dressed in his "formal attire" for greeting official visitors to his sanctuary, feeds corn to one of the thousands of his "pet" geese at the pond beside his home (ca. 1925). (Dr. R.D. Sloane)

over which Jack's orientation to wildlife shifted during his lifetime.

Jack's interest in nature began when he was a young child. The forests and creeks near his home were his classroom where he learned the lessons of nature, for he attended school a total of only three months during his entire life. His special attraction to nature soon blossomed into a love that attained the spiritual, mystical bond that Livingston describes as the essence of wildlife preservation. Later, when he confirmed his commitment to God, Jack's spiritual attachment to nature would take on a distinctively Christian bent:

> As I stroll through the woods, my heart bubbling over with intense interest, I set my moccasined feet down with a hush for fear I might disturb the stillness; I wait till the wind moans slightly through the pines before I venture to advance; for the whole atmosphere seems sacred and I want to advance as silently as the still small voice that is there just as certainly as is the voice that comes from the radio into the dining room of my man-made home.
>
> As I sit down safely on the dry moss of a decaying log, among the many profound thoughts that come to me under such conditions is this: Why are writers turning out so much fiction, when all of God's out of doors is loaded with mature fruit which has never been gathered?

Jack based his approach to nature and his sense of responsibility toward it on God's dictum in the Book of Genesis whereby man was to "have dominion over the fish of the sea, and the fowl of the air, and everything that moveth upon the earth." But Jack's religiously based outlook went beyond denominational dogma and doctrine; it was an individual spirituality that approached Livingston's ideal nature ethic characterized by "an unequivocal acknowledgement of the *whole* inter-relationship between man and nature . . . which would of necessity involve both intellect and intuition . . ." And Jack's forte was the ability to instill this attitude in others, both by the example of his fostering of nature and wildlife at his wild goose sanctuary and by his inspirational lectures across North America in which he extolled the benefits of man caring for nature, his fellow man, and his all-powerful Creator.

Jack Miner became the object of great public adulation in the 1920s and 1930s. His lectures were invariably sold out and his drawing power was even greater than that of many notable statesmen and politicians. All in all, it is estimated that during his thirty years of lecturing Jack addressed more people than any other single individual had up to that time.

His work at his migratory waterfowl sanctuary and his success with popularizing the notion and practice of conservation won him much recognition and many awards. He was considered one of the five most recognized men in North America in the 1920s—along with Henry Ford, Thomas Edison, Charles Lindbergh, and Captain Eddie Rickenbacker. In 1929 he received the Outdoor Life Gold Medal for the greatest achievement in wildlife conservation on the continent. *The Book of Knowledge* included Jack's biography among those of the "twenty great men and women of the world" in their survey of the early 1940s. He received the Order of the British Empire in 1943. And in 1947, three years after Jack's death, the Canadian Parliament unanimously passed a bill creating a National Wildlife Week to honour his memory.

From an illiterate hunter and brickmaker, Jack Miner rose to become a world-famous naturalist and renowned wildlife lecturer and author. That an individual of his humble origins and essentially shy nature could inspire others to take up the cause of conservation, and make it a part of their everyday life, is testimony to the ability of a person who believes in a cause to effect changes where he perceives there to be problems. And unlike the modern activist conservationists, Jack was able to accomplish such changes by enlisting the support of, rather than alienating, the rich and powerful, the politicians, *and* the general public alike. By examining the course of Jack Miner's life and the impact that he had on people, we can begin to appreciate that this man had been endowed with a unique ability to make his *experience* of nature meaningful to his fellow men and to convert them to the cause of conservation in the process.

. . . it is true that I have
never seen a human being
possess better eyesight and
hearing than I did, or one
who could slip through the
woods more noiselessly . . .

2

At Home in the Woods

J ACK Miner was born in Dover Center, Ohio, in 1865. He was the fifth of ten children born to John and Ann Miner, who had originally emigrated from Leicestershire, England. Although nine of the Miner children had been born in United States, the Miners were taunted for their foreign origins, and their taste for sturgeon meat cooked with mushrooms and home-grown savoury earned them the epithet: "English people that eat sturgeon and toadstools!"

As a boy Jack spent his time at the creek near his home instead of in the schoolhouse. That creek bed soon became both his playground and his classroom as he put in long hours studying nature's ways. He liked nothing better than to listen to the birds singing or observe the habits of the animals. In what was to become a characteristic curiosity, he studied the frog-swallowing prowess of snakes, the water-locating ability of snapping turtles, and the transformation of polliwogs:

> Another outstanding study of mine was those big polliwogs, or tadpoles. I would steal up, quietly, and watch them, with their noses out of those stagnant pools, as they were wiggling for life. Then I would scoop them out, pick out the larger ones, put them in my pockets and carry them possibly a quarter mile to some larger pool that was not so apt to dry up; there I would kneel down and, turning my pockets inside out, pick up each tadpole and pinch a tiny piece off his tail. In other words, I earmarked them at the switch end. I got absolute proof that polliwogs turned into frogs. Also, that the more I visited them, the less they appeared to fear me. And that the temperature of the water in which they were living did hasten or retard their development.

Jack received much support for his nature studies from his mother. While Mrs. Miner understood that he was losing the benefit of a formal education, she knew that the lessons he learned in the woods would stand him in good stead in the years to come: ". . . although I was only eleven years old, she could plainly see that I was doing my own personal thinking. Moreover, she was a real naturalist; and she knew that by studying Nature, I was not apt to study wrong . . ."

In 1905, Jack saw this drawing, labelled "Jack Miner at the Height of His Ambition," hanging in the railway station in Stralak, Ontario. It reminded him of his youth, and the station agent, Mr. Fulcher, gave it to Jack as a keepsake. (Miner Collection)

Overleaf: Jack "slips noiselessly through the woods" on a moose-hunting trip to Northern Quebec in November, 1897. (Miner Collection)

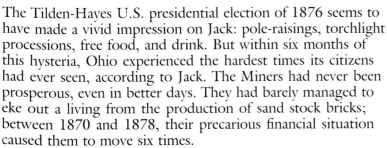

The Tilden-Hayes U.S. presidential election of 1876 seems to have made a vivid impression on Jack: pole-raisings, torchlight processions, free food, and drink. But within six months of this hysteria, Ohio experienced the hardest times its citizens had ever seen, according to Jack. The Miners had never been prosperous, even in better days. They had barely managed to eke out a living from the production of sand stock bricks; between 1870 and 1878, their precarious financial situation caused them to move six times.

In 1877 the Miners made plans to move north of the border to Canada, to join Mrs. Miner's kinfolk. The Broadwells had settled near Kingsville, a small town in Essex County in Southern Ontario. It was about twenty-five miles southeast of Detroit and was close to the north shore of Lake Erie. Prospects seemed better there and English folk more welcome, and on April 22, 1878, the family loaded themselves and their belongings into wagons for the day-and-a-half trip. Years later Jack would vividly recall that a neighbour's query as to whether they expected to make a living in Canada had evoked a profound, positive response from his father: ". . . we are going to make more than a living. We are going to make a life."

Their initial optimism proved short-lived. The cheap price Mr. Miner had paid for the hundred acres he had purchased was a result of the land being in the heart of a settlement of "colored people," offspring of slaves who had escaped from the South. While the Miners found these people to be good neighbours, the family soon learned that the hot, wet summer weather flooded the extremely level land with several inches of stagnant water, attracting what Jack described as "swarms of hungry flies and savage, bloodthirsty mosquitoes." Jack's baby sister soon contracted malaria and the local doctor advised them to move away for the summer lest all the children die. Forced to remain due to lack of money, Mr. Miner demonstrated a strength and determination that seemed to be a family characteristic. He located an outlet for the water, and he and Jack and Ted started ditching. Within a week they had done

Jack's mother (standing in the doorway) and his father (seated before the window) with other family members in front of their first log cabin home in Canada in the early 1880s. (Miner Collection)

A portrait of Jack's mother, Ann (née Broadwell), and his father, John, with Jack's oldest sister, Martha (ca. 1890). (Miner Collection)

enough to drain six acres. What could have been an unmiti- gated disaster was turned into a tremendous victory: "The ditch was completed, the water ran off, and all Nature seemed to back us up, for the big, heavy rains ceased, the woods dried up, and dear little sister got well."

With that problem overcome and initial alarm over the pres- ence of numerous rattlesnakes behind them, the Miners took to clearing the land in preparation for planting. They discov- ered two acres of choice soil close to their log house and Mrs. Miner was soon working her magic with the crops and flowers she planted. And Jack, of course, was thrilled by "the immense variety of so-called 'wild' creatures that were keeping the woods echoing with song and good cheer." By August 1, 1878, the homestead was no longer recognizable as the depressing swamp to which they had moved:

A portrait of Jack in his teens in the early 1880s with older sisters, Elizabeth (left) and Mary (right). (George Fields)

> . . . On three sides of it the virgin forest stood fully one hundred feet high, deeply clothed in summer foliage. The log house was all of one hundred feet from the road and the path that wound its way among the stumps to it was bordered on each side with mother's choice flowers, making it a perfect lov- er's path. The people came, even by waggon, "to see the flow- ers those Yankees have got." The stumps that were in our four- or five-acre cornfield were no longer visible; they were covered with the rank growth of corn. Indeed, I have never seen a more vigorous growth of vegetation in a glass hothouse than we had that summer.

The Miners were now relatively better off than they had been in Ohio. But when the weather turned cold and they could no longer grow their own food and they needed "boots, shoes, socks and good, plain, warm clothing," Jack turned to nature to supply their needs. Like many others who had to rely on their wits and wile to meet their families' needs, Jack became a market hunter.

First identified by this term in the early 1600s, this breed of tough, independent gunner used every trick in the book (and developed more) to slaughter as much game as possible. Ac- cording to American conservation historian James Trefethen, most hunted for profit by choice, taking pleasure in the free- dom that roaming the wilderness gave them. In fact, many were social misfits or outcasts who operated on the outer fringes of any hunting laws that existed. Moreover, in the mid- 1800s the railroads were still completing their push across the continent, bringing an end to frontier America, and the settlers and sportsmen who arrived in the West also engaged in the wholesale slaughter of birds and animals, for few grasped the concept of limits to the numbers of North American wildlife— and fewer still the notion of conservation.

Although he was never a market hunter of the most extreme kind described by Trefethen, Jack first realized the true poten- tial profit to be made from selling game during the Christmas

season of 1878 when his brother Ted secured some ammunition

> . . . and he and I went hunting partridge (ruffed grouse). I
> acted as dog and he did the shooting. We succeeded in getting
> about twenty birds and took them up to the old stage line,
> and that night the stage driver gave us four dollars in return for
> the twenty birds. This gave us the brightest of hopes and
> cheerful desires, and a real vision of what was to be during the
> next fall, when the hunting season opened again. The anticipa-
> tion of the next nine or ten months was beyond words.

That next hunting season a donated dog and a borrowed gun
produced a box of quail and grouse that fetched over ten
dollars and further increased the boys' interest. But the roots
of Jack's market hunting go back to his skunk-catching days in
Ohio. He had caught his first skunk and sold its pelt before
he was eight years old, and by age eleven, he was using the six
traps owned by the Miners to catch as much as five dollars'
worth of furs in a week—money that supplemented the family
income. Jack also used his skills to snare raccoons, foxes,
crows, ravens, and hawks to keep as pets—and to secure
enough food to satisfy his ravenous charges. In the summer of
1880, when his uncle George Broadwell gave him a hunting
dog and his father bought him a perfectly fitted double-bar-
relled shotgun, Jack's market-hunting career started in earnest.
And as he later confessed, the desire to shoot had been there
even before he could afford a gun and ammunition.

Equipped with a good firearm, supplied with ample powder
and shot by Ted, owning both a bird dog and a deer dog,
and armed with a vast knowledge of the woods and its inhab-
itants, Jack Miner became a market hunter of remarkable
prowess. In the autumn of 1882, however, an event occurred
that set Jack apart from other market hunters and foreshad-
owed the more fundamental changes in his life that were to
take place in the future. Despite objections from both his
mother and Ted, Jack had continued to hunt on the Sabbath.
While to others it was a day of rest as decreed in the Bible,
to Jack it was time free from work that allowed him to wander
farther afield to visit spots that were out of range during the
work week.

Then one Saturday evening in September, 1882, Jack was
visited by a neighbour friend who warned him that some men
were going to catch him hunting on Sunday and prosecute
him for violating the Sabbath. The news angered Jack greatly
and although nothing happened the next day, he detected men
following him during his hunting trip the following Sunday.
Jack took several evasive actions to throw the men off his trail
and doubled back to where their horse and wagon stood.
Having recognized one of the men's dogs and now the other's
horse, Jack felt a greater anger than he ever had before:
". . . never—never—in all my life, did my crimson disposition

burn wickeder . . ." Locating a buggy wrench under the back cover of the buggy, he began to take the nuts off the wheels when suddenly he was struck by feelings of sympathy and remorse. As a lump rose in his throat and tears trickled down his cheeks, Jack realized that the men were trying to help him rather than hurt him. He retightened the nut, replaced the wrench, and put eight of the black squirrels he had shot that day beside the buggy seat.

Arriving home early, he tearfully explained to his startled mother that he was never going hunting again on the Sabbath. And while he may not have recognized it at the time, he would later understand that God had cared for even an uneducated, barefooted skunk-catcher:

> For He laid His hand on me and melted my revengeful heart into love, yes, love for even the horse. And the blessed part of this whole happening is that I have had nothing but the warmest of loving feelings towards those two men ever since. Yes, I treasure the memory of them and of that blessed occurrence that changed my whole life's route. For from then on my thoughts were different, hence my desires were different and my ways different.

Despite this change in his routine, Jack continued to perfect his hunting skills and techniques. He loved his deer dog, Sam, greatly and was worried by the fact that the scarcity of deer had led many local deer hunters opposed to hounding deer to shoot dogs caught in the act. As a result, Jack wouldn't let Sam out of his sight, training it to trot just ahead of him and bark while he ran after it. Soon Jack and Sam were able to drive the deer in any direction Jack pleased, just as you would sheep. Jack claimed that the arrangement allowed him and Ted to shoot deer any time they wanted.

It was due to these skills that in the fall of 1882 a group of hunters invited Ted and Jack to go with them on a week's deer-hunting expedition. Embarrassed for her seventeen-year-old son because of his unkempt appearance and his lack of training to interact with "proper gentlemen," Mrs. Miner suggested that the men wanted Jack's dog, not Jack, and urged Ted to go alone with the dog. When Ted refused, claiming that neither he nor Sam were any good without Jack, Mrs. Miner relented and gave both sons permission to go. Once Jack overcame his own bashfulness at the prospects of the trip, arrangements were made to set out on a Monday in mid-November.

The hunting party consisted of five of Kingsville's most prominent and respected citizens: John J. Malott, the town's mayor, and Major Wagstaff, the township clerk and justice of the peace, along with Ed Pulford, John Carscadden, and a Mr. Burdick. Within a few hours Jack and his dog had located some deer and driven them toward the hunters, with Mr. Pulford killing one of the largest bucks any of them had ever

The men were amazed at Jack's ability to run with his

dog and never seem to tire, at the skill with which he butchered the downed buck, and at the speed and agility with which he wielded an axe to provide firewood for the hunting camp. The rest of the week was as successful as the first day. Each member of the hunting party shot at least one deer, and a total of seven were killed of the twelve sighted—the best deer-hunting record in which, Jack noted, he ever took part.

The party rewarded their guides with two deer in appreciation of their assistance, but Jack felt that the deer "were nothing compared to the kind respect these gentlemen had shown to us, two under-privileged young men." Major Wagstaff, in particular, took pains to compliment Jack, remarking that his work with his dog had been a revelation and that Jack had a beautiful future before him. Jack was pleased with the praise, but when he got Ted alone he had to ask him what "revelation" and "future" meant, for he had no idea. All in all, these five men had such a profound influence on Jack that he concluded ". . . to be treated and spoken to as those men treated and spoke to me made it almost seem that I was entering on a new life."

At about this time Jack began his transition from market to sports hunter. The experience with the gentlemen of Kingsville was a major factor; the improved economic fortunes of the Miners, as a result of the discovery of a good bed of tile and brick clay on the Miner property, was another. The distinction between these two approaches to hunting had been hazy until the mid-1880s, according to Trefethen. Men who shot game merely for pleasure had sold their excess, while most of those who killed game for profit had derived pleasure from their work. The wealthy hunters who could afford to hunt for satisfaction alone soon became exclusively sports hunters, buying up their own choice, posted hunting grounds to provide themselves with game unaffected by the relentless market hunters. It was not long before these sports hunters became concerned about the effects of unrestricted killing of game on future

A dealer in game stands beside three deer that Jack killed and sold to him (ca. 1885). (Miner Collection)

stocks and began to organize into groups that laid the ground-work for conservation efforts and the conservation movement itself. The earliest and most effective organization, by Trefethen's account, was the New York Sportsmen's Club, formed in 1844 by about eighty influential New York sports hunters (most of them lawyers). They sought to eliminate market hunting, outlaw the spring shooting of game birds, and tighten lax game laws; and to achieve these goals they drafted a model game law that was instituted in a number of counties in the state. According to Trefethen, the club "was so effective in its crusade against game-law violators that its approach was adopted before 1850 by newly formed groups of sportsmen in Boston, Massachusetts; Providence, Rhode Island; and Toronto, Ontario." By the outbreak of the Civil War similar organizations had been established in most of the major Eastern cities. Despite these developments, market hunters continued in their thoughtless exploitation of wildlife resources.

Jack's commitment to sports hunting was further strengthened in the winter of 1884 when he and Ted were invited to shoot with the Kingsville Gun Club. The club made them members, and the next fall the two brothers were invited to join the first Kingsville hunting party to Northern Ontario, organized by Mr. Malott, who had also led the deer hunt of 1882. It was on this outing that Jack saw his first moose head, a trophy of the postmaster of a small northern town. Jack was amazed that an ordinary bullet could kill such a monstrous animal, unaware that he would one day be as proficient in hunting this lordly animal as he was killing game birds, deer, and the other animals he pursued.

But this was not to happen for more than ten years, after Jack had married and started a family. In the winter of 1895-

Jack makes a pot of coffee outside his tent during one of his moose-hunting trips in Northern Quebec during the late 1800s. (Miner Collection)

96 he made preparations for a moose-hunting trip to Northern Quebec where, unlike Ontario, there was an open season on the animal. The next fall Jack took his younger brother, Amos, with him on an expedition to a remote northern section of Quebec. Jack found the novelty and unfamiliarity of the whole experience greatly exhilarating:

> . . . what made our moose-hunting prospecting doubly interesting was the fact that we had no guide whatever to take us to, or away from, the best hunting grounds. Better still, we were absolutely ignorant of the nature of the moose. In fact, all I knew about them was what I had heard brother [Ted] read out of this sporting paper [*American Stream*] . . . and that was so grossly exaggerated as to be of no value.

The tangible results of the hunt were less satisfying. While they killed a deer and as much partridge as they wanted, no moose were to be had. Amos wounded two, but was unable to kill them, and Jack merely caught a glimpse of one big bull. Nonetheless, the promising hunting ground they had located, and the firsthand information on moose habits they had gained, made the trip worthwhile.

Jack returned to the same spot in November of 1897, this time accompanied by Ted and two friends. The lessons of the previous year had been well learned and the first day out they killed a moose. From then on, his moose-hunting parties always were successful.

Jack studied these unfamiliar creatures just as he had studied birds and animals as a child, but his years of experience made his discoveries all the more profound and important. He saw in the hunter's approach to the moose more evidence that the word "wild" was more appropriately applied to man than the animals he feared:

> Of course when I first started to hunt them I found them very wild and hard to approach; but after I got to understand them, and got quieted down myself, I found they were not so wild. My fear of their getting away had caused me to do three times the shooting that was necessary; which, of course, made them afraid of me. That is what causes us human beings to say they are "wild."

He also combined his observations that the bull moose was one of the most sexually prolific animals on earth with the fact that cows and calves hid during the mating season in thickets that the heavily antlered bulls could not enter. This led him to conclude that the horns prevent the bulls from chasing after a cow and she takes advantage of that fact. And while Jack asserted that "I have no proof that our God, the only perfect Manager this world has ever known, put the horns on the bull moose to protect the mother in time of need," there is little doubt that this is what he actually believed.

Deterred from hunting by Ted's tragic death as a result of an accidental shooting during a hunt in 1898 (see Chapter 3), Jack declined to go north the next year with John Malott and his party. But he provided them with a map of the moose-hunting ground so accurate and easy to follow that Mr. Malott was moved to tell some friends that "Jack Miner can draw a map so plain that you could find, with it, a pen knife seven hundred miles away, in the pathless wilderness."

However, Jack resumed his hunting career a couple of weeks later, after being approached by another group of Kingsville sportsmen. He was finally persuaded to join them after receiving some fatherly advice from Mr. Miner, but he insisted that, to avoid being the cause of any accidents himself, he would never again go into the woods with another hunter. He followed this practice until years later when his own sons accompanied him.

Disappointed that his friends had not sighted a single moose on this trip, Jack made extra efforts to locate some of the animals to prove it was the good hunting ground he had claimed it to be. After a morning of noiselessly following tracks through the woods, he smelled the moose "just the same as you would smell a herd of cattle under the circumstances." He stole up close enough to see the animals, which were absolutely unaware of his presence, and sighted more moose than he had ever seen together at one time. Jack had mixed feelings as he drew a bead on this quarry, which he often called "bow and arrow" game. "The strange—and somewhat pitiful—part of the story is that when I raised the rifle and shot all the moose our party should have, the rest did not run away, but raised their long manes and stood around as quietly as so many domestic cattle—yes, or more so—until one, finally, gave a snort and then all that could, ran away."

The success of this annual big-game hunt soon became a fixture in Jack's life. The results were turned to good use because he had become a member of the Kingsville Cemetery Committee and the hundreds of pounds of moose meat from the hunt were turned over to them for annual moose dinners, called Klondike Dinners since they were organized at the time of the Klondike gold rush. The proceeds from these events, as much as 350 dollars one year, were used for the upkeep of the Kingsville Cemetery, which Jack claimed in a very short time "was converted from a rabbit-jungle into the most beautifully kept cemetery in southwestern Ontario, and other towns copied the example set by Kingsville."

The local sportsmen's admiration for Jack had first emerged as awe at his hunting and woodsman skills when he was a seventeen-year-old hunting guide. Now in his mid-thirties he was regarded as their leader, "our dear Gorilla Chief" as they called him in the citation that accompanied a silver bread plate presented to him in 1901. Jack, with characteristic modesty, said it was only then that he realized that he was looked

upon as their leader. On another occasion a different group presented him with a Bible that had special passages underlined. As he unwrapped the gift, the book opened to a page with these words, which burned themselves into Jack's memory: "For as by one man's disobedience many were made sinners, so by the obedience of one shall many be made righteous." Jack always treasured this memento of his hunting trips, the first book given to him after he became a man.

Kingsville is situated in a rather unique territory as regards the migratory routes of waterfowl. This southwestern portion of Ontario between Lake Huron and Lake Erie sits at the juncture of the very margins of both the Atlantic and the Mississippi Flyway—flyways being the network of migratory routes connecting the breeding and wintering grounds of waterfowl. Such a marginal location probably accounts for the scarcity of the Canada goose in the Kingsville area before the turn of the century, since it has been noted that this species exhibits a strong affinity for specific migration routes and wintering areas. But Jack did hunt these wild geese during this period and began to learn something about their habits.

A portion of Jack Miner's hunting trophy collection in front of the original family home in 1904. In 1915 Jack sold his collection to the Canadian Pacific Railway for the Pan-American Exhibition in San Francisco and it ultimately ended up in the Chateau Lake Louise at Lake Louise, Alberta.
(Miner Collection)

AT HOME IN THE WOODS **39**

In the 1890s a few Canada geese were landing about four miles north of his home. After several people approached him about going out to shoot these geese since no one had been able to kill one, Jack set about making decoys to lure the birds within gunshot range:

> Well that day I went home, took the axe and chopped out the bodies of three wooden wild geese decoys; then I used a drawing-knife for the rest of the work; finally I had three geese standing on one leg in our back yard—one leg each of course. And I had everybody who saw them laughing at me. What color should I paint them, was the puzzle. I had never been close enough to a wild goose to know anything about his color . . . I finally decided to paint their breast light and the rest a slate color. The neighbors still kept laughing. Then when there were no persons around I would practise the "Honk!" till the echoes from the buildings sounded something like it.

Assisted by his brother-in-law, Jack set out at two o'clock one morning to try to shoot his first wild goose. After locating tracks in an old cornfield adjacent to a wheat field, he set the decoys where the geese landed and dug himself a hiding place at the edge of the cornfield. Covered by a blanket the same colour as the ground, he lay in wait in his six-inch-deep trench.

Just at daybreak, Jack caught sight of a dark streak in the sky off to the south, and he readied his gun and himself for the upcoming test. It seemed ages before anything happened and at first he thought he had been mistaken. But when he gave out two of his best goose calls he was surprised to hear a low reply from the east. Looking in that direction, he saw eight geese and gave another low call. The geese turned and seeing the decoys, answered as they prepared to join them.

But as they approached, the gander saw that the decoys were false and veered away. Its path carried it in front of Jack, however, and in an instant he had shot both the gander and its mate, leaving the six young ones to fly off screaming in the direction from which they had come. It was then that Jack learned a few lessons about the Canada goose's appearance. "As soon as my chum arrived we had a good laugh when we looked at the decoys and the real geese. We soon loaded all up and could hardly get home quick enough to repaint those blocks of wood. Then they looked O.K., and fooled many a goose after that. . . ." But the Canada goose was not to be a frequent trophy for Jack: "I hunted geese every spring from then on, but they soon got wise and moved their stopping place about eight miles west to what was then called Walker's Marsh. I even followed them up there and secured an odd one now and then. I never killed over six in one season. This will give you an idea of how scarce they were in this part."

After the turn of the century, Jack's fame as a hunter had spread well beyond the local Kingsville area. In the summer of

1902 a stranger appeared at the brickyard inquiring for Jack Miner. He turned out to be a travelling passenger agent for the Canadian Pacific Railway and reported that he had heard Jack was "the greatest hunter in Canada." The CPR wanted Jack to take a railroad car of hunters north during the fall, and offered to send him up there whenever he wanted to scout for hunting grounds. Jack accepted the offer, and from an initial party with one passenger and one baggage car in 1902, the ranks swelled within two years to 180 hunters from Essex and Kent counties who occupied an entire train. Jack looked forward to these expeditions and the scouting trips that preceded them.

He eventually became more interested in the "living thrills" of conservation than in the "dead thrills" of hunting. He shot his last moose in 1917, but every fall he still felt compelled "to go and hide away for a few weeks in the stillness of the wilds." By the mid-1920s he was confining his killing to the predators of the wildlife he sought to protect; however, he never begrudged the true sports hunter his rightful share of fairly hunted game. And he was always positive about the impact that hunting trips could have on a person:

> I tell you, everybody, I know by experience that men can go out together and live in bunches, have a good, clean, cheerful outing, and come home the better men for it, with greater love toward their fellow men. By taking such a month, away, far from the grind of life, it gives body, heart and nerves a rest and allows the soul to develop. We become better sons, husbands and fathers in our homes, and better citizens of the neighborhood and of the town, township, county and country in which we live.

Furthermore, Manly Miner reports that in his father's lectures during his later years, Jack preached the virtues of fathers taking their sons on hunting trips with them: "He says, instead of going hunting this fall with that group of fellows, take your boys with you . . . [since] your sons and you can have a far better time."

Jack Miner had another less well-known but ultimately more impressive woodsman's skill: Based on what longtime friend Dr. J. Earle Jenner described as "his sense of location and · direction . . . akin to that of the denizens of the woods," Jack had the uncanny ability to locate people who had been stranded in the woods and given up for lost. All told, Jack was credited with saving thirteen lost individuals. The first incident occurred on his second moose-hunting trip to Northern Quebec in 1897, when he was accompanied by Ted and two of their friends. One member of the party left to wait for the mail and return to the camp the next day, while the other three split up to pursue the moose. But at the appointed rendezvous time in camp the next evening, Jack and Ted were left waiting

Jack (left) and three fellow sports shooters relive the pleasures of the hunt (ca. 1895).
(Miner Collection)

for their two companions. A lack of response to some warning shots he fired into the air stirred Jack into action.

Jack setting out to look for one of his companions who had become lost in the woods.
(Miner Collection)

He secured some food, a lantern, and a pistol from the tent and set out while Ted remained at the campsite. Soon finding the tracks of the friend who had been out hunting, Jack followed them easily until the unhappy event he had anticipated transpired: It began to snow. By half-past eleven so much snow had fallen that he could no longer follow the tracks and he became increasingly concerned. His frantic shouts brought only echoes in reply. It was then that Jack invoked his religious faith:

> . . . With an aching, troubled heart I stopped under a big hem-lock tree, where the snow wasn't falling quite so fast, and there I poured out the whole situation to God Almighty, and asked Him for help. . . . I promised my Heavenly Father that if He would only assist me so that I might find those two men and take them to their loved ones, I would never ask another man to go into the wilds with me again. . . . And I closed my petition to the Almighty God by saying, "Oh God, I am going to depend on You." Then, just as I raised the lantern to start up again, I heard a gun, straight south of me, in the distance.

Jack had been headed in the opposite direction but now he changed course, shouting his friend's name as he ran, and finally he heard a faint reply. Soon he was reunited with his soaked and exhausted friend. The man's eyes were bloodshot and his voice trembled as he spoke, and Jack quickly recognized that he must be kept moving so that his physical condition would not deteriorate further. So, while he felt he could easily have carried both the man and his rifle, Jack bullied his friend into following him as he gradually increased the pace to a near-run. Stopping only once to give the other man some food

Jack got him back to camp shortly after 6:00 A.M.—a full five hours after they had been reunited.

Ted had been watching for them the entire night and quickly served up a breakfast of boiled moose meat and vegetables. The friend was unable to eat but Jack wolfed down a few panfuls of it, and before long both men were bedded down inside hot flannel blankets. But Jack was not to get the sleep he needed and deserved because after a couple of hours, Ted roused him to report that there still was no sign of the other friend who had been left waiting for the mail. The snowstorm had worsened and the temperature continued to drop, and the two Miner brothers knew that something had to be done immediately. Jack knew the woods better than Ted did, so he put on Ted's dry clothes—his own were still too wet—and after another hurried meal he was off again before 10:00 A.M.

After setting his course and travelling several miles in deep snow, Jack came upon a current-ridden lake, the last one he had to cross. Deciding that skirting the lake would be too time-consuming, he fashioned two poles about twenty feet long to help him traverse the frozen surface safely, holding each in his bare hand so that he would have some chance if he did happen to break through the ice. After completing the treacherous journey successfully, he had to free his hands, which were frozen to the icy poles. He trudged on, still hampered by the extremely deep snow and weighed down by the ice that had formed on his clothing, until he sighted a track leading back toward a settlers' house that the Kingsville men used as their headquarters during their hunts. As Jack recalled, "Although I still had six miles to go and I must make it that night, with a faint hope that all might be well, I asked God for strength and guidance and pushed on."

But the weather worsened as night fell and finally he lost his way. When the clouds broke he found himself in a clear field, and after crossing the next hill, he saw the dim light of the settlers' home and knew he was out of danger. Once inside, he found his friend safe and sound, telling everyone that he had known Jack would come after him. Jack, almost delirious by this time, collapsed into bed. Having spent almost twenty-four hours of the last two days in the woods, most of it at night in a howling storm, he slept late the next day. But by afternoon he was back at camp with his three companions.

Two years later on another hunting trip Jack again demonstrated his remarkable knowledge of the woods. In mid-afternoon, while he and a friend were butchering some moose he had shot, he heard rifle shots in the distance. Knowing what the signal meant, Jack was, as he described it, "nerved up to the highest pitch at the thought of someone lost." He heard nothing further as he trekked through the woods until his shouts brought a rifle shot in reply and he quickly located a party of hunters that had been stranded in a blinding snowstorm the previous day. Among them was Dr. King, who had

treated Jack's baby sister for malaria when the Miners had first moved to Canada. He was in a bad way, unable to walk and with purple lips and face. Acting as if he was going to die, he gave instructions as to what his three sons should be told.

But Jack would have none of that talk. Unable to get Dr. King to stand, he instructed the other men to put their companion on his back, and with his compass as a guide he set out in the lead with the others following him. Reassuring Dr. King as he went, Jack demonstrated his legendary strength and endurance as he toted the 185-pound man back to camp. "I do not know, to this day, whether it was my strength or the excitement that made it so; but the fact is he was not heavy, and I almost ran with him. In fact, I went so fast with him that the other men stacked their guns against a tree in their efforts to keep up with me." When they reached camp, the efforts to restore Dr. King were successful.

The "big joke" of the evening, as Jack called it, occurred when he asked the whereabouts of the guns since they would be wet and must be cleaned. It was then that the men realized that they had left their four or five valuable rifles behind as they hurried to keep up with Jack. Given his familiarity with that area of the woods, Jack ended up going back to retrieve the rifles with the help of one of the hunters. But as cheerful as ever, he made his way there and back to the camp in time for a second moose-meat dinner that night.

Another gripping rescue took place several years later in 1909 when Jack took his entire family with him to Northern Ontario in order to try to get away from hunters altogether. He had reached the point that, whenever he was in the northern woods and heard a gun fired at night that sounded anything like a signal shot, he would be unable to get back to sleep. He hoped that camping with his family and hunting with his boys would restore the peace of mind that he usually experienced in his contacts with nature. But on this particular occasion it was not to be.

One day Jack had taken his young sons out in hopes of having them shoot a moose, but an injury to one of the boys curtailed these plans and, as they headed back to the railroad, Jack saw his wife talking to some railroad section men. When she informed him that a boy had been reported missing farther along the rail line, it seemed to Jack that "every nerve in my whole body was at its highest tension" since it was not a man who was lost but a *boy*. He grabbed some provisions and hopped a passing express train, which dropped him off near where the boy had last been sighted.

There he met a group of seven or eight boys whom he questioned about their lost friend. He learned that the young-ster, whose name was Tommy Faught, was wearing moccasins, which would make him harder to track. He explained that Tommy had become lost the previous day because the train whistles, which he had expected to guide him, had been carried away from him by the strong north wind; the boy had become excited as a result and started running in the wrong direction, as lost people usually do. After giving them his second compass and telling them to stay in pairs if they went into the woods, Jack set off due north at a run. The weather was fine and the terrain was not too rugged; consequently he was able to keep up his initial pace for at least an hour. Three or four miles from the railroad, he was in the heart of the wilderness—in an area with which he was unfamiliar—and he felt as if he were searching for "a lost diamond in a thousand acres of pebbles."

Jack continued northward, calling out Tommy's name but getting no reply. To help strengthen his resolve and sharpen his powers, Jack turned his attention to the entity whom he had always credited with making his dramatic rescues possible:

> With tears almost running down my cheeks, I tried to pull myself close to Almighty God, and asked Him for guidance. Yes, it was not even a silent prayer. It was uttered aloud, in my backwoods worded way: "Oh, God in Heaven, my strength and life-long knowledge of the woods is absolutely useless without Your aid. You, and You alone can direct me to him. Oh Heavenly Father, please do this. Don't let this boy die in the woods, but guide me—oh, guide me—oh, guide me to him, that I may take him home to his loved ones."

His prayer brought no inspiration to change course until the bloodcurdling howls of timber wolves to the north convinced him that no purpose would be served by continuing in that direction. Jack then decided to return to his family rather than spend the whole night in the woods. At daylight he would take a handcar ten miles farther down the rail line and continue his search for Tommy.

Darkness set in and when he reached a lake at about seven o'clock, he decided to build a fire rather than join his family that night. But not able to find an appropriate spot, he kept on, his thoughts absorbed by his own predicament. Suddenly he realized that he hadn't called out Tommy's name for quite some time. To his amazement and delight, his shouts were rewarded by the shouting and screaming of a boy not more than 300 feet from him. But once he had informed the boy that Jack Miner was the name of his would-be rescuer, he received no further response.

Only later did Jack learn that Tommy, in his delirious condition, had mistaken Jack's name for that of the Grey Fox, Bill Miner, a noted highwayman and train robber of that period. Having apparently read exaggerated novels about this other man, Tom thought that old Bill Miner was after him and became frightened, so he stopped answering Jack's questions. After making sure the boy was all right, Jack fired the agreed-upon four signal shots, and then he and Tommy made their way to the railroad, guided by a bright star above them. After a short, joyful ride on a handcar back to the station, Tommy was given a hot bath and a light meal and put to bed by Mrs. Miner. Early the next day he was on his way to a reunion with his anxious parents in their nearby home town.

Tommy brought Jack a present three days later; Mr. Faught sent a letter expressing the family's undying gratitude. Jack took great pride in Tom's accomplishments as an adult and the two often visited during Jack's annual trips north. On occasion Tom even travelled to see the Miners at their home. But while Jack was pleased to have been able to help out, he felt he was only the vehicle for the purposes of a higher power. ". . . I am sure you will agree with me when I say it was not I, at all, who found that boy. Very true, I produced the effort and strained my whole being in the attempt; but we must give God the credit. He *did direct* me to that boy."

Dr. King was also grateful to Jack for his rescue, but Jack vowed never to take advantage of his friendship with this wealthy man. Moreover, he was deeply offended when he overheard a man in Kingsville telling others that Dr. King would not have tried to save Jack if the situation had been reversed. For Jack, what he had done was simply what any decent, God-fearing man should do: "If I have any manly principles about it, and if God has given me strength to help a man who is down, what right have I to hesitate a minute to use that strength to lift him up? What right have I to hesitate a second to consider whether or not he would do the same for me? Let me ask all classes: What did the good Samaritan do?"

Jack's curiosity about and love for the natural world took different forms throughout his life, depending upon the circumstances and influences he encountered; but they were always there nonetheless. During his childhood they motivated his innocent explorations of the woods. They helped him turn his

A few days after his rescue Tommy Faught poses for a photo, dressed in the same shredded clothes he was wearing when Jack found him lost in the woods in 1909.
(Miner Collection)

knowledge of the woods to the economic advantage of his struggling family during his youthful market-hunting career, and to the pleasure and camaraderie of the sportsmen of Kingsville, who made him one of their own. And combined with some significant developments in other spheres of his life, Jack's fascination with nature was destined to transform him into one of the most influential conservationists the world had ever seen.

. . . aside from its
unavoidable sadness, I have
had one of the most
beautiful, mysterious lives
that could be dreamed of.
Yet the full development has
often come only in the
eleventh hour.

3

An Awakening Consciousness

IN 1886, when Jack Miner was twenty-one, the word "conservationist" had not yet entered the lexicon and would not do so until the dawn of the twentieth century. As for the possibility that someday Jack would become a popular wildlife writer and public speaker, there couldn't have been a less likely candidate. Jack's brief encounter with formal education had done little for him; he couldn't read or write. He was still so shy that he rarely spoke to people at the best of times. And, of course, his remarkable hunting prowess was the most telling argument against such outlandish speculation. But no one could have envisioned the events that would dramatically alter Jack Miner's life and force him to reconsider the meaning and purpose of his existence.

In retrospect, his transition from hunter to conservationist, covering the years 1886 to 1905, has a certain logic to it that resembles a relatively straightforward jigsaw puzzle or the familiar cause-and-effect relationship of a tumbling row of dominoes. But certainly none of Jack's later success would have been possible without his tremendous source of inner strength as well as his seemingly visionary quality—his ability to look at "the big picture" based almost exclusively upon very specific firsthand experience.

And there are other factors that give Jack's story a curious twist. The location of Jack's home—on the outer edge of the Atlantic and Mississippi flyways and not more than twenty-five miles from the capital of America's industrial empire, Detroit—played a significant role in his development as a conservationist. Even his early brickmaking career had a major part in Jack's determined efforts to halt the relentless pressure of progress-oriented North America upon the declining wildlife population. For those who believe in such things, Jack Miner seemed destined for greatness.

Jack had been involved in the manufacturing of brick and drainage tile for as long as he could remember. When he was six and living in Dover Center, Ohio, his father had given him an ultimatum: Go to school or work with him in the brickyard. Jack had chosen the brickyard.

Overleaf: The Miner clan in 1896. Jack is standing to the far left beside an unidentified bicyclist. Ted Miner is standing one row back, between Jack and the woman. Jack's wife, Laona, is seated in the front row (right) with her daughter, Pearl on her lap and son, Carl seated beside her. (Photo courtesy Robert Kennedy)

The Miners produced sand stock bricks and baked them without the aid of a kiln, on the brickyard grounds. As soon as the sun and wind had dried the exposed sides sufficiently, the bricks were turned on their edges. This became young Jack's first job. Each morning at breakfast his father would announce that he had a few thousand bricks to edge up. "All I need to have said was, 'Father, I want to go to school.' But, no sir! I was willing to do anything rather than face the pointed fingers, sneers and laughter."

By the age of eleven Jack was "as hardy and strong as a wildcat," fully capable of taking a man's place in the brickyard. Even after the family moved to Canada, Jack remained a brickmaker. The first few years he worked with his father at a relative's yard. Always the outdoorsman at heart, the boy took advantage of the long walk between his home and the Broadwells' factory to cut through the bush, where he could carefully observe the abundant wildlife that still flourished in the county.

> Could any teenage boy have a more healthful or beautiful dream than my life had automatically drifted into? There I had from three to five hours a day wandering through the virgin forest, visiting and studying all the creatures that lived there as I rambled back and forth to and from my work. Often I would leave home before father was out of bed; and before I reached our clearing again in the evening, I heard the hoot of an owl in the distance . . .

While his deep love of nature was the most important reason for Jack's daily adventures, it was not the only one. He suffered from a deep self-consciousness about his appearance, and for a good reason. His face was a mass of freckles and his wild, unruly red hair was very long because it was cut but once a year. His floppy old hat, seatless jeans, and bare feet would have been the envy of any clown. But, worst of all, Jack was anointed with a vile-smelling potion given to him by an old coon hunter to ward off mosquitoes. He was probably doing everyone a favour by sticking to the woods.

When he was seventeen Jack and his brother Ted started their own brickmaking business on property rented from a neighbour. The dense forest of Essex County was slowly being cleared for farming and people began moving into the area in large numbers once it was discovered how fertile the land was. Homes, businesses, and schools were sprouting up throughout the county and the need for quality building materials did not go unnoticed by the Miner brothers.

The first two summers were very profitable for Jack and Ted—perhaps too profitable. "Our brickyard profits . . . not only bought us the best of footwear and clothing, but assisted in erecting barns on the farm at home." When their landlord heard of their success he refused to rent the land to the Miner brothers the following year and he went into the brick business himself.

Jack and Ted were not out of work for very long, however. In the spring of 1884, as they carried on clearing their own property, Ted discovered a huge deposit of clay, a brick- and tile-maker's motherlode. The brothers broke out their shovels and were quickly back at their trade, selling more than ever.

Their brickyard operated from early spring until late fall. In 1889 "the Lake Erie and Walkerville Railway (now operated by the Pere Marquette Railway Company) really opened up Kingsville. Brother Ted and I got orders for three hundred thousand brick. We wisely discarded our one-horse machinery, and replaced it with up-to-date steam power." The operation was growing and five men were hired to help meet the demands and operate the machinery. Now much of the winter was spent cutting the 400 or 500 cords of wood needed to fuel the operation.

The work in the yard suited Jack's nature. Never one to shy away from physical labour, he worked long, tough hours digging and hauling the thousands of pounds of clay. He was outdoors, where he always wanted to be, and in this business he was, literally, close to the earth. In keeping with his need to be alone with his thoughts, Jack especially loved those long, quiet nights when he had to tend the kiln as it baked the bricks to a durable consistency. "The sky above my face looks bluish-black, illuminated with thousands of twinkling stars, and each is staring right at me. There I am—*alone*. I pick out a space

Jack, in the middle of the group, poses with some of his employees at the Miner brickyard (ca. 1900).
(Miner Collection)

between four bright stars and try to count the dimmer ones in that small area."

As the business prospered and more people began to come out to the yard to get their orders filled, Jack became comfortable with the world beyond his muddy realm. Ted—certainly not one to ignore Kingsville's social life, particularly when there was a dance to attend—began coaxing his brother to take part and eventually talked him into coming along. One of Jack's favourite social events was the barn raising. People from around the area would gather, in the pioneer spirit, to help a neighbour erect this important edifice. Jack's experience as a tree climber ("to get to pigeons' and crows' and hawks' nests") made him a great favourite "as my bare feet never made a slip but clung to the newly hewn timber like a tree toad to an apple tree."

One Sunday in February, 1886, the Miner brothers decided to attend a local Sunday evening revival meeting at the nearby schoolhouse. What happened to Jack at this get-together reads like something that only Hollywood could have envisioned. As the choir began singing, a young girl leading the group caught Jack's attention. Ted noticed his younger brother's fascination and prodded him into getting up and joining the singers. Jack was the hit of the revival meeting. He tried to head for the exit in his usual shy way but there were too many people between him and the door, all seemingly interested in thanking and welcoming him. Before he knew it, the curly-haired girl from the choir who had piqued his interest was among the others giving thanks.

Jack couldn't forget the revival meeting and the young choir leader, and finally, with Ted's encouragement, he overcame his feelings of inadequacy and began visiting the girl who had caught his fancy—"I had almost worn a beaten path from our log house down to this brick house . . ." Her name was Laona Wigle, daughter of a prosperous Kingsville couple, and two years later, on December 24, 1888, they were married.

The newlyweds began their life together in a rather peculiar fashion, though somewhat appropriate for Jack. During their first winter they lived with Laona's family but, as the weather warmed the following spring, Jack and Laona set up house-keeping on their own under the fragile protection of a large canvas tent. A few months later the young couple moved into the white clapboard house that Jack had built beside the yawning clay pits of his brick and tile yard.

In the spring of 1891 the Miners' first child, Carl, was born. Three years later a baby girl, Pearl, became a welcome addition to the Miner household and, like most daughters, she was the apple of her father's eye. As soon as she could toddle, Pearl became Jack's constant companion, trailing behind him as he worked in the brickyard. She often took her afternoon naps

out by the machinery, and Jack, who doted on her, would carefully cover her up with his jacket as she slept.

Perhaps because he now had a family of his own, Jack began to feel pangs of guilt about his market-hunting days. His earlier conversion from a gluttonous mercenary to a responsible sportsman had apparently not eased his mind. In 1895 Jack decided to try his hand at raising English, or ring-necked, pheasants. "Having often heard father speak of the English pheasant as a beautiful game bird, and as I was overly anxious to pay Canada back some of the birds I had murdered in my younger days, I decided to try these pheasants." Though this bird was not indigenous to the area, Jack felt that it could survive the relatively mild climate of southern Canada. But not one of the pheasant eggs hatched. Fortunately his mother had been given some eggs, too, which she put under one of her hens, and eleven of them hatched. Jack wisely adopted her method and the next time he was successful.

As happened with most of his ventures, Jack's dabbling quickly evolved into a serious undertaking. He set aside four acres of land and enclosed all of it with a tall wire fence. This became his pheasant farm. Inside the enclosure he built several brood pens and put one male pheasant and five females in each. Jack shrewdly continued to use chickens to hatch the eggs, putting about twenty eggs under each of the hens. This freed the pheasant hens from their normal maternal chores

Jack looks uncomfortable in his suit as he poses with Laona for their wedding photo in 1888. (Miner Collection)

Jack and Laona's first child, Carl, born in 1891. (Miner Collection)

and they "laid from thirty-five to fifty eggs between April the 15th and June the 15th." Always the great experimenter, he tried various combinations of feed for them until he came up with the best one possible. "In this way I stocked this township so I could have shot two bushel bag full in half a day. Two miles north of my place there were twenty-eight seen dusting in the road at one time." Jack was so successful at raising pheasants that he not only stocked the surrounding counties but also shipped more pheasants into the United States for propagation purposes than all other Canadians combined.

In September, 1897, the Miners added another child to their brood. They named their new son Manly after Jack's close friend and brother-in-law. With three young children in the house Jack no longer spent all of his spare time in the woods, but this new family way of life gave Jack a different kind of contentment.

However, on one October day in 1897 his and Laona's happiness was shattered and an ongoing cycle of misfortune

Mary Pearl Miner, born in 1894, with her pet dog and rabbit. Photo was taken in 1897. (Miner Collection)

Carl, Jack, baby Manly, and Laona in 1898, posing with a portrait of Pearl, who had died the year before.
(Miner Collection)

and bittersweet hope was begun. Three-year-old Pearl contracted a mysterious fever and died a few hours later. Jack was devastated. ". . . as strong as I have been all through my life, it seemed I could not gather strength to leave her grave. Only those who remember when they faced death for the first time in their own family circle can have any conception of how heavy our hearts were. We finally went back to our little place called home. But it wasn't home."

Once again the natural world became a refuge for Jack. Although he was still consumed with grief, his family convinced him to resume his annual hunting trip with Ted and two friends. It was on this trip north that Jack risked his life to locate these two men, who got lost during a freak snowstorm. It proved to be a harrowing way to take his mind off his own troubles.

By the following spring Jack's spirits were revived and his family gave him a great deal of personal satisfaction. His oldest son, Carl, was growing up to be a remarkable child. Jack taught him to target-shoot and the boy, though hardly as tall as his rifle, quickly mastered the sport. Laona encouraged her son's musical talent and Carl progressed rapidly at the violin.

In the fall of 1898 Jack eagerly prepared for his moose-hunting trip north with Ted. That year the Miner brothers decided to take along their friend and brother-in-law, Manly Squire, the namesake of Jack's youngest child. They travelled by rail and boat to a remote area of Quebec near Beauchene Lake. The brothers were eager that their friend shoot a prize moose on this, his first trip north with them. The first day was a big success. Two moose were killed. The following morning the three men woke up early, ready to pursue even bigger quarry.

Carl Miner's prowess with a rifle was well documented.
(Miner Collection)

. . . after a hearty breakfast of moose heart, we started back to skin our other moose and prepare the meat for carrying out. Squire's gun did not work right that morning; two shells would come up instead of one. I saw him working with it and I said, "What's the matter with your gun?" He said it is all right now, Jack, as he clapped it together.

Jack went on ahead toward the other carcass but he decided to veer off course, hoping to discover another moose. Ted, aware of his brother's habits, alerted Manly to the possibility that Jack might locate another moose. Jack's hunch was correct: He soon came upon a huge bull moose and drove it to a predetermined location where Ted and Manly waited. Suddenly Jack heard shots ring out—four quick ones, a pause for about thirty seconds, then two more in rapid succession. Jack ran ahead, anticipating a successful kill.

. . . Then I was terrorized as I heard a voice ring out, "Oh my God, Jack!—Oh my God, Jack!—Oh my God, Jack! I have killed your brother!" No human tongue could ever express the feelings these mournful shouts brought over me. . . . I ran up the road as hard as I could and there, about one hundred steps from the lake, right where we had planned they should stand, lay my dear brother, his face downward in the snow. I at once took him in my arms, washed the blood from his mouth with a handful of snow and spoke to him as I did. Yes, and I kissed him. But he was dead.

As expected, the moose that Jack startled had fled right to the spot where Ted and Manly waited. In order to escape, the animal had charged the two men who were blocking its path. Manly, no doubt as fearful as his quarry, fired four shots in an attempt to shoot the onrushing giant. His rifle jammed before he could finish off the wounded and enraged creature. Ted stepped into the breach and killed the charging moose but, just as he fired, Manly's rifle accidentally discharged, striking Ted in the back of the head and killing him instantly. Ted had saved Manly's life, but in doing so had lost his own. Though stricken with grief, Jack gathered all the strength left in his 165-pound frame and proceeded to carry the body of his 200-pound brother out of the bush and back to civilization, some twelve miles away.

On November 19th, 1898, we laid my dear brother at rest beside my little girl in the Kingsville cemetery. And it was at our dear friend's request that the following inscription was carved on his monument,

> "Greater love hath no man than this,
>   to lay down his life for a friend."

. . . .

The man with the little bit of education was gone. The balance wheel was gone. To me he had been a father and a brother combined, and we had not been apart ten days in our lives. But then I would have to be without him, always.

Ted Miner's grave.
(Calvin W. Moore)

After a heart-to-heart talk with his father, Jack realized that
his only recourse was to carry on with his life and get back
into his work. He hired a couple more men for the brickyard
and they all spent the winter months cutting the hundreds
of cords of wood needed to run the steam engines during the
summer operation. Laona took over the bookkeeping for the
business. Despite their efforts the brickyard did very poorly
that summer.

Jack spent a dreary winter pondering the fate of his business.
But his bad luck quickly reversed itself one January morning
in 1900 when a telegram arrived at his home: A large farming
operation in nearby Walkerville, Ontario, needed all the drain
tile he had available. The cheque that followed, for 4,000
dollars, was the largest he had ever seen. "Although I was over
thirty-three years of age, that was my first occasion to go into
a bank."

This surprising windfall paid off all of Jack's debts and allowed him to buy up more of the surrounding property. Still,
he was puzzled by the fact that he had received an order from
a company that had never done business with him before.
After some investigation Jack discovered that his benefactors
were business associates of Dr. King, whose life he had saved
while hunting in Quebec. Jack's bravery and kindness were
being paid back. This big sale brightened his life considerably
as his brickyard began to return a modest income.

In the spring of 1900 the Miner family was blessed with the arrival of a baby boy. Jack named him William Edward (Ted) in memory of his late brother. But, in a way, the appearance of another Ted in the household only increased the memories of the original one. Jack suffered from bouts of melancholy whenever he started thinking about the past, for his brother had played such a prominent role in it.

Carl recognized his father's profound unhappiness and sought a way to ease the pain. Each Sunday, when the rest of the family went to church, Jack remained at home caring for his infant son. On one of these occasions Carl suggested to his father that he come along to church with the rest of the family. After much persuading, Jack agreed to go along. It was a decision that forever changed his life.

As he sat in the far corner of the church, taking care of the baby, Jack observed a group of restless boys disturbing the congregation. Eager to put an end to the disruptions, Jack offered to take charge of the young troublemakers by putting them together in a Sunday school class, which he would oversee. The following Sunday he began his class. He was quite firm with the boys although his physical presence alone caught the attention of his charges.

William Edward (Ted) Miner in 1903.
(Miner Collection)

> About the second Sunday we got together, little George jabbed the other fellow with a pin, which caused quite an explosion. I was on my feet at once, and I put a regular meataxe look on my face and gave a few grinds of my well-preserved teeth, then started talking to them in plain, backwoods English, giving them to understand that they were not in Mrs. Johnson's class, nor Mrs. Jane's class, but in Sunday School; and that they had to behave. In the same voice I added that nine of us could be part of the Sunday School; we could make it or break it. Then, pressing my question firmly home to them I said, "Which would you rather do, make it, or break it?" By this time I had them all seriously thinking.

Jack still had one major obstacle to overcome—he couldn't read and consequently his knowledge of the Bible was limited. He realized that his only alternative was to speak about the things he knew best: his experiences with nature. He asked the boys to select and read biblical passages that related to nature study; then Jack, as a follow-up, led a discussion based upon what he knew. His countless tales of adventure and discovery fascinated his young audience and they began inviting their friends to come to hear Jack and his stories. During the summer his class visited his home and Jack took them out on excursions to the nearby woods to observe the creatures that inhabited it. In return for his kindness and concern the boys gave Jack a precious gift:

> Yes, God bless them! they taught me to read. You see, we would start with a Chapter and read verse and verse about. Of course I had to skip my verse, till the little fellows said, "Come

Jack poses with his Sunday school class in 1910.
(Miner Collection)

on Uncle Jack, we will help you." . . . Those dear boys helped me spell my way through my verse, and got me interested. How could I help being interested? For what we were reading out of the Good Book of all books, corresponded exactly with what I had discovered and knew to be true; yet I had never dreamed such things were promised us in the Bible.

Literally, from the beginning, Jack discovered that the Bible was a tremendous source of hope and inspiration. The first book, Genesis, sparked his imagination and rekindled childhood memories. Chapter 1, verses 26-28, told of God's creation of "man" in His own image and His plan that man and woman should "be fruitful and multiply, and replenish the earth, and subdue it." Jack paid particular attention to the word "subdue." He read on and discovered that God's message was even more specific: "Let them have dominion over the fish of the sea, and the fowl of the air, and everything that moveth upon the earth."

As he studied these verses by the light of a lamp during his evening watch at the brick kiln, Jack reminisced about his family's early trials in the Canadian wilderness. By subduing the land, clearing the trees, and draining the stagnant water, the Miners had survived and prospered. As a young boy he had witnessed the disappearance of the passenger pigeon, once the most abundant bird on the continent. He had heard many tales about the buffalo slaughter in the West. As a successful market hunter he had seen at first hand the result of uncontrolled killing upon the local game, and now he concluded that this practice on a continent-wide scale would cause the wildlife population to decline. Through man's interference the game population had been steadily decimated and, conversely, only through man's intervention could that population be maintained or increased.

Jack believed that his early childhood experiments, his pheasant rearing, and even his market-hunting career had unconsciously been confirmation of the biblical pronouncement. With that strong and, to Jack, unwavering declaration for all mankind, the course was clear: Man had a responsibility to wildlife. The line "Let man have dominion over all" would eventually become the bedrock of Jack's philosophy and compel him to devote his life to wildlife, mankind, and ultimately, his God.

Reading further along in the Bible, Jack discovered what he considered to be the first game law.

> I found in Deuteronomy, twenty-second chapter, verses six and seven, which reads as follows: "If a bird's nest chance to be before thee in any way in any tree, or on the ground, whether they be young ones, or eggs, and the dam sitting upon the young, or upon the eggs, thou shalt not take the dam with the young: but thou shalt in any wise let the dam go, and take the young to thee: that it may be well with thee, and that thou mayest prolong thy days."

Jack was able to test this bit of wisdom when, the next spring, a pair of swallows visited his brickyard. Rather than shoo away these valuable insect-feeding birds, Jack allowed them to build their nest in the long drying shed, far removed from the noisy end of the factory where the machinery operated. When the swallows' nest was destroyed by their enemy, the English sparrow, "I went up in the air pretty high and came down with a .22 rifle in my hand . . ." The swallows rebuilt their nest and raised a family of four before disappearing during the fall migration.

"The next spring two pairs came back, one pair occupying the old nest, but the others built about fifty feet closer to us [at the other end of the factory]." Jack made it a point to protect the birds whenever their enemies threatened them, and ". . . it seemed that the swallows called to us as much to say 'Help! Help!' whenever their enemies put in an appearance, and I always tried to be on hand like a sore thumb." As the years passed, the swallow population around the brickyard increased dramatically and, as a result, there was a noticeable decrease in the fly population. "Now scientists tell us that these typhoid flies will carry germs. Such being the fact, when this bird catches and devours the fly that is on its way to your house with the dreaded disease, then it has prolonged your days. 'That it may be well with thee, and that thou mayest prolong thy days.'"

Jack's ability to read broke down a tremendous barrier to his personal development. He was now open to the world of ideas, a world not bound by time or space, and the more he read the more he realized that there were others who shared his concerns. A friend mailed Jack a copy of *Rod and Gun in Canada*, a sporting magazine, and he read a short article on the decreasing game. The article struck a nerve, and so, in about 1902, he attempted to organize a local game protective association.

> . . . remember, I am of a determined make-up and nothing knows this better than the game I pursued in my younger days. Finally, the annual meeting time arrived and I was cheerfully greeted by a bunch of real live, determined gentlemen, chiefly from Leamington, Walkerville and Windsor, and in less than two hours the leadership of this little existing association was in the hands of some real live, educated gentlemen, whose hearts and souls were of one accord. The Essex County Game Protective Association was thoroughly organized . . .

While it was important that all members of society learn about the declining numbers of wildlife, Jack and his associates took their campaign to those who really had a significant role to play in the survival of the game population: the hunters. They needed to learn about the consequences of reckless and wasteful hunting practices—shooting the female of any species before the young were born or killing five or more wildfowl a day per hunter. To compound the problem, market hunting on a large scale was still in vogue and it would continue to be a sore point with all conservationists until the first quarter of the twentieth century. A grass-roots organization like this would hopefully influence hunting practices in the area, and in turn it could bring about the creation of other organizations that (in time) would effect real legislative action with respect to game laws.

Jack's new efforts were not without their detractors, particularly those who recalled his prolific market-hunting career.

A 1915 photo of the Essex County Game Protective Association. The president, Ed Kerr, stands second from the left; the secretary, Forest Conover, is seated second from right; Jack is in the second row, sixth from the left.
(Miner Collection)

"An insulting doctor once said to me as he stood in the safety zone and shook his fists at my red face, 'Jack, you are just like old Uncle Joe; when he used to dance he wanted everyone to dance, but when he got religion he wanted everyone to pray.'" In spite of much local criticism, the Essex County Game Protective Association carried on and each year the small but determined group held its annual meeting at Jack's home.

Although it might seem paradoxical that a sportsman like Jack Miner, regardless of his circumstances, would become involved in wildlife protection, it is not unprecedented. John F. Reiger in his book *American Sportsmen and the Origins of Conservation* argues that the earliest conservationists were, in fact, sport hunters and anglers.

> Increasingly, gunners and anglers looked upon themselves as members of a fraternity with a well defined code of conduct and thinking. In order to obtain membership in this order of "true sportsmen," one had to practice proper etiquette in the field, give game a sporting chance, and possess an aesthetic appreciation of the whole context of sport that included a commitment to its perpetuation.

Reiger also contends that "conservation, at least, began as an upper-class effort." Only those with wealth, social standing, and political clout were able to enact legislation to set up national parks and maintain wildlife. President Theodore Roosevelt is the most obvious prototype of Reiger's conservationist/sportsman. Hunting and fishing for these men, Reiger adds, were leisurely pursuits, and because they had no direct economic ties to their quarry, they maintained a "distanced" perspective. The larger middle class portion of society still had no time for such activities. Although Jack himself was not a member of the upper class, he was friendly with many of the wealthiest and most influential men in the area, and their turnout for the Essex County Game Protective Association supports Reiger's contention.

Something other than money separates Jack from Reiger's concept of the early conservationists: his spiritual perception of the relationship between man and nature. John Muir, the founder of the Sierra Club, was similarly motivated. Hence Jack was willing to forgo the pursuit of material rewards ("the only bank account I ever had was an overdrawn one") and devote much of his life to conservation.

Jack continued to look for other, more tangible ways of helping to maintain the game population. Duck hunting had always been one of Jack's favourite pastimes and many of his memorable hunts involved these birds. "But, as I grew older, ducks, like all migrating birds, got scarcer until I seldom ever went to hunt them." In April, 1902, Jack managed to secure some wild duck eggs and he succeeded in raising three of them. This was the beginning of a modest attempt to increase the duck population in the area. In later years his efforts increased significantly, but his transition to wildlife conservationist was not complete until he learned a lesson on the plains of Cottam.

In the spring of 1903 Jack spotted a family of six Canada geese passing by his home. This was a rare sight indeed, for these elusive birds had been completely avoiding this part of the county for the past few years. Jack figured that they were headed to their old feeding area, about four miles from his house, near Cottam, Ontario. The next morning Jack gathered up the decoys he had made some years earlier, hitched up his buggy, and raced out in hot pursuit. He located their tracks in the snow on a field outside Cottam, as he had surmised, and he set up his decoys. He constructed a goose blind for himself by staking down an old blanket. "The sun is just high enough to be making golden windows in the distant houses to the west of me when I look to the south and a short, dark line appears in the sky. It is geese, sure; and they are coming straight this way."

Jack's hopes were quickly dashed when he spotted two men from a nearby farm crossing between him and his intended victims. Much to his surprise, the geese did not veer away in alarm; they kept their course and headed straight for Jack and the decoys.

> As they came over the field that I am in, a call comes from under the blanket, "A-honk!" and the old leader replies, turning my way, feet to come down. But just before they get in range of my deadly aim, this cunning old father's voice suddenly rings out in the morning air, "Khonk! Khonk! Khonk! Khonk!" These sharp, alarming danger-cries are given in rapid succession, and every goose darts for his life. Their terrified cries can hardly be described. They finally fall in line again and fly back towards the lake.

In all his years of hunting he had never seen anything like it. This amazing confrontation profoundly affected him and he thought deeply about what had happened. He concluded that somehow the geese could tell that he was someone to be feared. After all, they had flown directly over the other two men without any qualms. They must have been the same geese that travelled by Kingsville each year, for they went to the same locations annually. As a result they had learned to regard this redheaded gentleman hunter as an enemy. Jack was intrigued. "To be frank, I studied wild geese until I felt like flying. Surely they must be the same geese. They do know me as an enemy. No man on earth knows their cunningness and depth. If they know me as their enemy, surely they would know a friend if they had one."

Jack, by now totally consumed by his fascination with these wily creatures, devised a plan to befriend the wild goose. He located a man in the county who trapped Canada geese and he bought seven wing-clipped birds from him. He then flooded one of his brickyard pits and placed the birds in it. Jack figured

These are the original seven pinioned geese that Jack placed on his brickyard pond (ca. 1907). (Miner Collection)

that by using a tame flock as a decoy he could attract other geese to his home. Realizing that his plan would work only if he got full cooperation from his neighbours, he told them about the plan and he also told them ". . . if they would not shoot at the wild goose around here I would bring some right to that place and we would shoot a limited number when the opportunity was right." He felt that if they were given the opportunity to shoot a few, his friends would be satisfied and, hopefully, the geese would not be so alarmed that they would never return. However, all of this was wishful thinking because no geese arrived, and none was spotted in the spring of 1904.

Jack's frustration in trying to attract the wild geese was reduced to insignificance later that summer when his eldest son was stricken by the then deadly killer, appendicitis.

Fatherly pride notwithstanding, Jack recognized that Carl was a special lad. The boy's marksmanship was well known; he was becoming a very proficient violinist; and at the age of twelve he had taken over the bookkeeping of the brick and tile company from his mother. Manly can recall times when his very resourceful, considerate, and mature brother used to take him (then age seven) and three-year-old Ted to Detroit for his music lessons. They would hop aboard the old electric train and travel twenty-five miles to Windsor, proceed by ferry across the Detroit River, and catch a streetcar to his music teacher's home. Following the lesson, young Carl would treat his brothers to some ice cream and then the three would retrace their route to Kingsville.

A 1903 photo of Jack's boys, left to right: Manly, Ted, and Carl. (Miner Collection)

Carl had taken ill with all the symptoms of appendicitis, but for some unknown reason he was not operated on for nearly two weeks. By then it was too late and Carl's death was only a matter of time. "He was perfectly rational up to the last paroxysm, and had said several days before his death that he could not get well, and talked freely of the heavenly land he expected to reach." Carl invited his Sunday school teacher and his classmates over, thanked them all, and bade them farewell. He then thanked the doctors and nurses who had attended him. Finally Carl said goodbye to his father and mother.

... he gave me the most beautiful talk I think any father ever heard. I said to him, "Carl, lie down now, and be quiet and go to sleep." Then, with his head on the pillow, he looked me straight in the eyes and said, "Papa, I am going to sleep, but I am not going to waken here." Then, raising his hand, he added, "Papa, please don't cry, you have nothing to cry for. You have been a good papa to me. Oh, papa, how I would like to have lived so I could have paid you back for some of your kindness." And again he said, "Papa don't cry. Be kind to mama and the little boys, and Nettie who lives with us, like you have been to me, and meet me in Heaven, won't you papa?" I couldn't stand it; and as I backed out of the room my darling boy whispered, "Good-bye papa, good-bye."

Carl's funeral (in 1904), like most funerals of the time, took place in the family home. (Miner Collection)

Carl Miner, age thirteen, died August 21, 1904, and he was laid to rest beside his sister Pearl and his uncle Ted in the Kingsville cemetery. Once again a family tragedy left Jack emotionally devastated. Jack called upon his newly renewed religious faith to help him endure his personal anguish but, deep down, he couldn't understand why such a supposedly loving God could bring such grief to his family and cut down a youth of such exceptional character.

Manly Miner never forgot his father's despair following Carl's death. "Well do I remember going to town once a week and he took the family, Ted and I, to the church that we attended and he and mother would kneel in prayer at the altar, asking God to help him." The sudden deaths of three close family members in seven years would be traumatic for anyone, but for someone as highly emotional and loving as Jack, the loss compounded upon loss was incalculable. Fortunately, his uncompromising faith (thanks to Carl), which had in turn crystallized his life's work, allowed him to clearly rationalize and accept the tragedies that had befallen him.

> There is one thing God in Heaven gave to you and me, that He never takes from us. Yes, He can lay His powerful hand on your loved ones and take them, one by one; yet the way I see this today is that they are only loaned to us for reasons known to Him only . . . There is one thing God gives us that He never takes from us. That is our will. We can have a path of roses, or of broken glass and thorns. This He has left for us to decide.

This portrait of Jack was taken ca. *1904, after the loss of his brother and his two children.* (Miner Collection)

We have demonstrated what a man with no natural advantages and very limited means can do alone; what can the people of North America do for these God-given creatures with their combined forces?

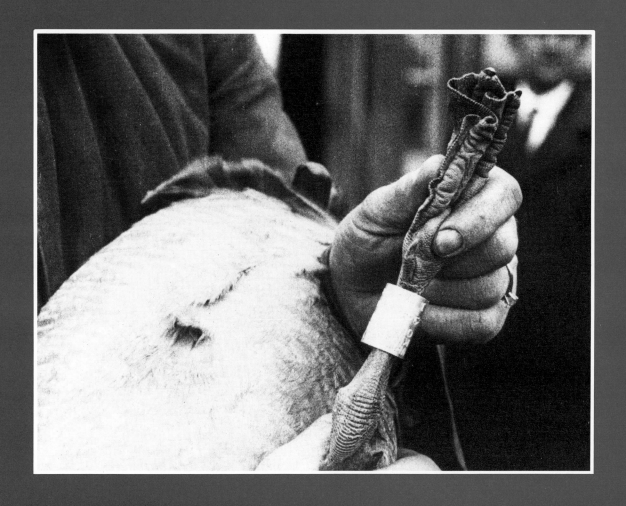

4

Success Is a Journey

IN the early part of the twentieth century Thomas Edison
and Henry Ford epitomized a unique spirit that enveloped
the entire continent, not just the United States. This was
the last great age of the "rugged individualists" and Edison's
immortal line that genius consisted of 10 percent inspiration
and 90 percent perspiration implied that opportunity was there
for the taking. One's dream could indeed come true—if one
were willing to work for it. You didn't have to be wealthy.
Education wasn't a factor either. Before the success of Edison,
Ford, and others like them ironically transformed society into
a "technocracy" (symbolized by highly educated, anonymous
scientists and less-educated, interchangeable assembly-line
workers), the world was ripe for self-styled innovators.

In 1904, as he neared his fortieth birthday, shy, reserved
Jack Miner, the brickmaker from Kingsville, Ontario, gave no
indication that he was out of this same mould as Edison and
Ford. However, like them, he had a practical grounding in the
ways of the world (the natural one in this case), and he most
certainly had a dream that he could somehow affect, if even
in a simple way, the creatures that inhabited it. Jack had no
idea that his modest successes would create such a furor and, in
turn, force changes upon his own life. Even with his lack of
formal education he was about to become widely recognized
as an "expert," sought out by highly educated specialists for
his opinions.

As the bird sanctuary that he created grew to be one of the
showcases on the continent, Jack literally became a one-man
conservation movement. His lifelong shyness notwithstanding,
Jack grasped the opportunity wholeheartedly, for he always
had within himself a burning desire to share his knowledge
with others. Some of his devotees were the most influential
men in the world, both wealthy philanthropists and powerful
politicians. Jack captivated these people with his honest, self-
effacing personality, his genuine love for his fellow man, and,
most of all, his contagious enthusiasm. It was through these
important contacts that Jack was able to bring his ideas forward
and into the boardrooms of policymakers. A 1929 editorial

*Overleaf: Jack holds one of his
banded geese. Throughout
his lifetime he banded about
50,000 birds.* (Ford Motion Pictures, Miner Collection)

in the Ottawa *Citizen* perhaps best summed up Jack's influence upon the conservation movement of the day:

> Let it be granted that others before Jack's time, and during the generation that has grown up since his experiments began, have done much good work in the same line. Yet, it remains true, in this as in every form of advance, that one person stands forth in the public eye as embodying the whole movement. Not Watt, but a succession of inventors made the steam engine; not Bell, but the electrical experiments made the telephone. Jack Miner, in this sense has given us the bird sanctuary.

However, it was scorn, not praise, that was heaped upon Jack twenty-five years earlier as he tried to realize his dream. The Jack Miner Bird Sanctuary was officially created in 1904 with very little fanfare and absolutely no takers. The Canada geese failed to visit Jack's home that first year and they also declined to make an appearance in the spring of 1905. The notion that the geese would land in the autumn wasn't even considered, for they had rarely been spotted during that time of the year.

Manly Miner can vividly recall those lonely days when the only comments directed at his father were derisive as people openly mocked Jack for his hare-brained scheme. "We used to go to town on Saturdays to do our shopping. As soon as we would arrive in town, the people would honk at him. And, of course, that made me feel a little bit humiliated." Jack kept his legendary redheaded temper under wraps whenever the townsfolk questioned his intentions because he had great faith in his plan after a lifelong preoccupation with the habits of God's creatures. Certainly it was only his deep-seated faith that motivated Jack, for there were no precedents for this type of sanctuary.

Neither the American nor the Canadian government had ever attempted to lure birds or animals to a previously uninhabited area in order to establish sanctuaries. The traditional policy was to set aside land already inhabited by the wildlife for the exclusive use of these creatures. But, as of 1904, even this policymaking had rarely been invoked.

Nature writer and filmmaker Janet Foster notes in *Working for Wildlife*: ". . . the first bird sanctuary in North America had been created by the federal government in the Northwest Territories (present-day Saskatchewan) in 1887. The islands and eleven miles of shoreline around the north end of Last Mountain Lake, fifty miles northwest of Regina, were withdrawn from settlement and set apart as a breeding ground for waterfowl."

However, Foster emphasized that the creation of this sanctuary did not signify a popular movement for bird protection by either the Canadian government or the public. "Rather, it was the result of one prominent individual's concern. Edgar Dewdney, the Lieutenant-Governor of the Northwest Territories, feared the extension of Last Mountain Lake Railway would bring in settlement and development that would destroy the area's natural wildlife habitat." Only following the passage of the Migratory Bird Treaty, some twenty years later, would the Canadian government become more involved in the creation of sanctuaries.

Meanwhile, in the United States a more concerted effort to establish wildlife sanctuaries was initiated following Theodore Roosevelt's rise to power as the President of the United States. A longtime sportsman and avowed conservationist, Roosevelt introduced policies that were revolutionary for the time. As in the Canadian experiment, Roosevelt's actions involved setting aside land that was already inhabited by wildlife and making that land off limits to hunters. James B. Trefethen noted that "On March 14, 1903, Roosevelt issued an executive order setting aside Pelican Island [Florida] as a federal bird reservation. This was the first unit in the National Wildlife Refuge System that eventually would encompass nearly 40 million acres." Yet even these measures did not resemble the type of work that Jack Miner was trying to carry on. In essence, he was attempting to create a refuge from literally nothing.

The spring of 1906 found Jack and his live decoys once again waiting patiently for the arrival of their first guests. Once more there was great disappointment. The spring of 1907 was a replay of the previous three since not one goose was lured or even sighted flying past Jack's corn-laden pond. There was no guarantee that the geese would ever come.

"But April the second, 1908, was my innings, for the whole neighborhood was aroused long before breakfast. The geese have come! the geese have come!" Eleven Canada geese had landed in Jack's pond. According to Manly, "He came into the house clapping his hands saying they've arrived and, I say, we couldn't hold him from going downtown to see who was doing the honking now."

While it might have been made four long years earlier, the neighbours hadn't forgotten Jack's promise and they soon arrived at his home, guns in hand, prepared to shoot some wild Canada geese.

> Now I had to face another serious problem, but all listened to me as I explained that if we did not shoot at them until they got settled down and made this their spring home, the ones we did not kill would return next spring and surely bring more with them. Every hunter was very reasonable, and, after having a quiet chat, each took his gun home. In about three weeks I hoisted the signal and every one was on deck. . . . All of us went over to the tile factory and watched these eleven geese from the upstair window until the goose fever got a few notches higher than our nerves. Then we all came down and marched up behind the embankment. "Now", I said, "don't shoot at them sitting, or you will hit my tame ones." Then I said, "Cock your guns," and I gave an alarming, "Honk!" and that instant every one of the eleven geese was in the air, and "Bang; Bangety! Bang!" went eight guns into them. When the soft

coal smoke had finally cleared away, five geese lay dead on the muddy water. The other six, screaming with fright, flew away to the lake.

Jack's gesture of goodwill appeased his neighbours, for each of the five nearby homes received a prize Canada goose. Unfortunately, the price he paid was a steep one because now the future of his sanctuary was in doubt. Jack could only hope that the survivors of the barrage would return the following spring. Much to his surprise, however, the geese returned about two hours later, "circling in the air and honking for their lost companions. Finally, they went away, but the next morning they were back, bright and early, and to my great satisfaction they lit and fed with mine, and it was surprising how soon they quieted down. I asked the neighbours not to shoot at them again that spring and all kindly agreed." The geese stayed at the Miner home until the first of May.

Jack felt that his long-awaited success would not be fully realized until the next year, when a pattern for arrival would have been established. Once again, as the spring of 1909 approached, Jack found himself the brunt of local jokesters who sarcastically asked for the date of arrival for his feathery guests. "But feeling confident I would be able to laugh last, I just gritted my teeth inwardly, and smiled from the outside, and answered as kindly as I possibly could." Fortunately, Jack did not have to put up with his doubting critics for long.

Sunday morning, March 18th, 1909, the ground was frozen as hard as Pharaoh's heart. I was out watering our own self-starter. While she was drinking out of the trough I was putting in time talking to one of my pet geese which were not over thirty yards away. All at once they all started honking at the top of their voices and acting extremely strange; but in spite of

Jack feeds corn to his tame birds. (Miner Collection)

their chatter, when I pricked up my ears I could hear strange geese honking, and looking over my right shoulder I saw something that caused my heart to fairly jump. There was a string of Canada geese, with wings bowed, coming right towards me.

This was the scene at Jack's pond when the geese made their second visit to the sanctuary in 1909. (Miner Collection)

Thirty-two geese landed in the pond: Apparently the six survivors had brought some friends along. Again, several gun-toting neighbours came over to "collect" their share. Ten birds were killed and, once more, the survivors, twenty-two in all, returned to the pond and stayed as welcome guests until May 1. Even his staunchest critics had to concede that Jack's sanctuary—the first of its kind on the continent—was now a reality.

Although Jack's experiment with Canada geese had been the focal point, it had not been his only concern during the early days of the sanctuary. He had maintained his interest in ducks and each year he had managed to raise a few. The wings of the brood stock had been pinioned or clipped to ensure their year-round residency and the young were sold to sportsmen, who used them as decoys. Not surprisingly, the arrival of migrating Canada geese in 1908 changed Jack's attitude toward this questionable practice.

Instead of selling the ducks, Jack allowed them to fly freely around his home and in the fall, following their instinctual habits, they went away. "The next spring several black mallards dropped in the pond and acted and looked for all the world like the ones that had gone away the previous fall." Jack initially doubted that the ducks could be the same ones. These birds, more than most, would have been easy prey for hunters because they had not developed a fear of man. And yet, when female ducks and their families started walking right up to the Miners' front gate, seemingly asking for safe lodging, Jack couldn't help but conclude that somehow these birds had remembered the location of his sanctuary. Jack decided to find the answer.

He singled out a female black duck that had landed in the pond on August 5, 1909, and patiently tried to approach his skittish subject.

Finally, she was eating out of the long-handled spoon that I had previously used for throwing little feed over to her. The spoon, of course, was on the ground, gradually being drawn towards me until it came over my left hand that was lying flat on the ground, and on September 10th the same year this duck actually ate out of my hand. We named her Katie. In a few months Katie got so tame she would follow us in the barn where we went after the feed. So I scraped around my hunting case drawer and found a piece of sheet aluminum about three quarters of an inch wide and one and a half inches long; then I took my sweetheart's best pair of scissors, and with pointed blade I managed to scratch my post office address on it. Then I caught Katie and wrapped it around one of her hind legs.

Katie was last sighted on December 10 as she headed for parts unknown. However, near the end of January, 1910, Jack received a fascinating letter from W. E. Bray of Anderson, South Carolina. Bray acknowledged shooting Katie on January 14 and, following more correspondence, he mailed the band back to Jack. While he still hadn't proved that ducks returned to their homes, Jack had made a significant discovery about the migratory habits of his birds.

Two years later Jack resumed his experiment. He stole four eggs from a black duck and set them under a domestic fowl. Familiar with the tendency of newly hatched ducklings to "bond," Jack set himself up as stepfather to the young birds. Later that spring he drove down to Detroit and bought a sheet of aluminum as well as a set of stencils. When the ducklings reached full growth, "each was presented with a leg band stamped with the following inscription: Write Box 48, Kingsville, Ontario!" Jack named them Polly, Delilah, Susan, and Helen, and on December 5 they disappeared on their fall migration.

Following the return of Polly (left) and Delilah in 1913, Jack took them to Kingsville for portraits. (Miner Collection)

A man from nearby Chatham, Ontario, reported that he shot one of Jack's four ducks (Helen) the following day. "But to my delight, on March 10th, 1913, Polly came home and on the 18th, Delilah came home; and although badly crippled in the wing and leg, Susan came squawking down out of the heavens on March 30th. I caught each one and examined their tags; and for the next three months I did all I could to induce people to ask me how I knew that birds returned to their same homes, for I had double proof."

Ironically, it would be the failure of his birds to return home that would give Jack much more valuable information, for returning birds would only reconfirm his early hypothesis. As hunters responded to Jack's request and wrote to him about downing his tagged ducks, he was able to chart the migratory habits of the birds. Jack banded a few geese as well, but he found them more difficult to catch and tag. It would be several more years before his bird banding became a significant part of his activities and played an important role in the formulation of conservation practices by Canadian and American government officials.

By this time Jack was completely committed to his conservation activities and his sanctuary was developing into a living testament to his faith in the biblical pronouncement that man shall have dominion over all. The third year of the arrival of the Canada geese in 1910, highlighted by the influx of 400 birds, marked a significant change in Jack's plans. "I got sanctuary fever." With all the activity and excitement associated with feeding and protecting such a large number in the spring, Jack felt uneasy and lonely during the quiet summer months. "Yes, I was forty-five years old and homesick for scenes and trees and sweet song birds, birds of my boyhood days. There was a robin heard in the distance as they issued their challenge to all-comers but outside this bird-life the summer was dormant."

There was little wonder why the Miner property was so devoid of life during the summer months. Thirty years earlier, the pioneering family had dutifully cleared all the trees off their property in order to create open land for the brick business and modest farm. The brickyard mudholes, particularly during the spring rains, reduced Jack's property to the barest and ugliest piece of landscape in the area. Acting upon advice from his elderly mother, Jack sought to remedy this woeful state of affairs—"I took on a new life." He secured some seedlings and proceeded to plant thousands of trees: He was sure they would attract the birds he so fondly remembered.

Always a student of nature, Jack copied its plan. He began by planting large numbers of evergreen trees and, although they were not indigenous to the area, he managed to make them grow in the densely packed soil. Amidst rings of evergreen trees he planted deciduous trees. This combination provided the birds, in winter, with a sun-flooded open space, surrounded by an effective windbreak. In another field he planted a great semicircle of red cedar and as they grew, the birds were afforded protection as well as nourishment from their berries. He cultivated other kinds of fruit-bearing shrubs and vines, all suited to the need of the many varieties of song and insectivorous birds that inhabited the surrounding county.

The winter of 1910 also marked the arrival of a rare bird; one that had not crossed Jack's path in a decade: the stork. Accompanying this bountiful creature was a redhaired, freckle-faced baby boy. Jack named him Jasper Wilson after a local minister and he constituted what Jack and Laona called their third family (following Carl and Pearl, then Manly and Ted).

The sanctuary was once again a popular mecca for the geese in the spring of 1911 and their number seemed to be increasing exponentially as each year passed. "On February 20th, 1911, they started coming from the South again, and in less than three weeks there was a small cloud of them. Really I did not know there were so many Canada geese on earth." While their numerical strength overwhelmed him, it was their strength of character that captivated Jack. Time and again he

observed heartwarming examples of the loyalty and bravery that seemed so much a part of their nature.

All around the border of Jack's property lurked eager hunters, desperate for a prize catch. Since spring shooting was still legal, Jack was powerless to prevent the hunters from firing upon the birds, and the geese were left to reach the protection of the sanctuary on their own. Not all the victimized geese died instantaneously from their wounds; many were gravely injured but, through some unseen force, they struggled to seek refuge at Jack's home. In *Jack Miner and the Birds* a story is related about one of these injured geese.

Jasper Wilson Miner at age three with his pet robins (1914).

Little Jasper, who was then three years old, was outside playing. Running in the house he said to his mother, "Mamma, goose out there; goose out there, mamma." His mother saw by his looks and actions there was something out of the ordinary, so she went out with the little tot and he pointed under a spruce tree, the boughs of which touched the house. And there, the goose, with her wings spread, lay dying. They called me from the factory, but when I arrived it was stone dead. On examination, I found a buckshot hole under the wing and it was evident that her "powerhouse" was punctured. The clotted blood on her foot proved to my satisfaction that she had been shot fully five minutes previous to dropping. Then I traced the blood back from where I picked her up and found that she lit within ten feet of our back door, for there, on the brick wall, was a big splash of her blood. In a few hours, I found that this goose was shot over five miles away.

On another occasion a big Canada goose was fired upon and one of its wings pinioned by the shot. The crippled bird and the rest of its companions eventually found refuge at Jack's home. They rested and regained their strength at the sanctuary until the first of May, the traditional departure date. However, as this one small group took flight, the crippled bird remained on the ground. One of the other geese spotted its flightless companion and flew back to the pond. There it remained with its wounded comrade. Jack dubbed them Jonathan and David.

> Dear old Jonathan! How he would get David to back clear across the pond, then run against the wind and try to fly! Yes, I have seen this happen fully twenty times a day; Jonathan would fly across the pond, but when he saw his brother David was not coming he would alight and swim back to him. . . . When fall came, we thought possibly Jonathan might go south, but no; neither our cold zero winters nor the extremely hot summers could drive him from his brother.

It was following this moving display of loyalty and devotion that Jack, in 1911, decreed that no more shooting would be allowed on his property: His neighbours would never again be allowed to "harvest" their share with his blessings.

The stories of Jonathan and David, along with tales of many other interesting geese, soon became part of the Jack Miner lore. Local newspapers began to publish articles about Jack's amazing home and his intriguing guests. The sojourn of the Canada geese was becoming one of the county's annual rites of spring. In 1914 a Detroit newspaper featured Jack in a Sunday rotogravure section, highlighting various activities at the sanctuary.

But now this increasing publicity was having an obvious effect, for the growing popularity and affordability of the automobile was producing a larger-than-ever number of curious visitors. Among those who saw that rotogravure in 1914 was the creator of the people's car, the Model T, Henry Ford.

Ford was an ardent nature lover and he enjoyed reading nature books in his spare time, particularly those written by the American naturalist John Burrows. Burrows once wrote of Ford, "His interest in birds is keen and his knowledge considerable." But Ford had taken his interest beyond the realm of most hobbyists. When he learned, in 1912, that a significant new piece of legislation affecting migratory birds, the Weeks-McLean Bill, was under consideration by the U.S. Congress, Ford sent one of his own advertising men, Glen Buck, to lobby for the bill. This action by a major industrialist significantly altered the minds of the legislators and eventually the bill, renamed the Migratory Bird Act, was passed in 1913.

Henry Ford sought out Jack Miner in the spring of 1914 and the two men quickly struck up a warm and lasting friendship. Some have speculated that their deep respect for each other sprang from the mutual recognition of a kindred spirit. They were approximately the same age (fifty) and both of them had achieved success by defying the odds and fulfilling their dreams, regardless of what others may have thought. In his own way, each man was wealthy. Henry Ford became a life-long supporter of Jack Miner.

But, apart from the increasing publicity and new-found friendships, the former laughingstock of Kingsville was still little more than a local curiosity. However, as Jack was wont to say: "There is no such thing as a man's life lying dormant. He is either advancing or deteriorating." Jack was definitely moving on, looking for new challenges. During the winter of 1914 he stumbled upon a new activity to channel his seemingly boundless energies and this, as much as the creation of the sanctuary, vaulted him into the spotlight as a conservationist and, moreover, as a human being of international acclaim.

> One Saturday afternoon in the fall of 1914, I was standing in a shoe store in the town of Kingsville, conversing with two gentlemen, when a plainly dressed Salvation Army lassie approached us and, holding out a small roll, said, "Buy a calendar, gentlemen; buy a calendar?" I happened to be the last one to refuse. But, as I shook my head, I glanced at the situation: We three men, all wearing good, warm overcoats, and this girl dressed in what I would call a summer suit. I spoke to her just as she was turning away. She at once whirled, her face beaming with smiles as she held out her paper roll towards me, as I dropped a quarter in her other extended hand and carelessly pushed what she had sold me into my outside overcoat pocket.

A few days later Jack noticed a beautiful picture hanging on the dining room wall. Apparently it was the calendar that he had purchased, for Laona had found it in his overcoat pocket. Upon further investigation Jack discovered that the calendar featured a selected verse for each day of the year. "This was the first one I read, 'From this day I will bless you.' I then studied one after another of them until I had read and re-read dozens and dozens of those encouraging promises, that seemed to fill the whole room with heavenly bread right from God's own oven of love." Jack was so moved that he sought a way to pass on these inspirational messages to others. First he put them into a booklet and gave them out as a Christmas greeting to friends. But a few weeks later he conceived a much more imaginative way of sharing his faith.

Jack's epiphany occurred late one night, near the end of the drain-tile season, as he took his customary shift tending the kiln. During the quiet moments Jack would sit back, stare up in the heavens, and search out the dimmer stars as he slipped deeper into thought.

> Just then I heard the swish of wings of a flock of ducks, and their low quacking as they dropped into the pond about two hundred feet away. At that moment one corner of my mind's eye had apparently drifted over to the three hundred and sixty-five blessings I had bought off the Salvation Army lassie for twenty-five cents, and, like a star shooting across the heavens, God's radio said: "Stamp these verses on what is now the blank side of your duck and goose tags."
>
> I threw the blanket off my shoulders and jumped to my feet. For that minute I had my tagging system completed.

Jack demonstrates his band-making technique. Each letter and number had to be stamped by hand. Jack produced thousands of these (ca. 1924).
(Dr. R.D. Sloane)

Opposite: This photo sequence documents Jack's prowess as a bird bander. He sneaks up on the geese, careful not to disturb them; then he pulls the trip wire to close the sides of the trap. Once the geese have quieted down, Jack rounds them up into the holding pen. With some volunteers, he places bands on the birds and notes those previously banded (ca. 1924).
(Ford Motion Pictures, Miner Collection)

The bird banding had once been a hobby; now Jack approached it with all the fervour of a crusader. Although each letter on every band had to be stamped by hand, and although the Canada goose was a particularly wily bird to trap for banding, Jack persevered. He spent many hours out by his pond devising a better goose trap. He achieved modest success initially and managed to trap and band a few birds. Almost immediately, during the summer of 1915, Jack discovered just how significant this new gesture had become.

The native people of northern Canada were the first recipients of Jack's greeting of brotherhood and love after the first catch of banded geese and ducks left the Miner sanctuary in May. Jack received a letter from the Hudson's Bay Company Post at Moose Factory dated August 19, 1915. A goose had been killed by an Indian in the unsurveyed territory of the Hudson Bay district.

As they shot the Canada geese for food, native hunters discovered that some of the birds had a strange band of metal around one of their legs. Eager to discover the meaning of the bands, the natives took them to their local missionary. The missionaries read the messages on the bands and explained that these were biblical verses. For those of Christian faith this was the word of God.

Many of the native people believed that these messages had come directly from God and several northern communities exploded in a rebirth of religious fervour—the greatest religious revival that missionaries had seen in thirty years.

Jack's new venture had far-reaching effects throughout the continent, not just in the north. As the birds proceeded south to their winter homes in the United States, many banded geese and ducks were shot by hunters. When they discovered these mysterious and often inspiring messages, the hunters reported their findings to the local press. It wasn't long before thousands of people who weren't even sportsmen learned about Jack's missionary geese. Letters poured into the Miner home. Some were written by those who had shot one of Jack's birds, but many others were from people who had never seen a Canada goose. They were simply moved by Jack's method of sharing his faith. "One duck, killed in Louisiana, brought to my home thirty-nine interesting letters of inquiry. Among them was a letter from the Arkansas State Prison."

The letter was written by an inmate who had been imprisoned for passing a bad cheque. He and his cellmate, a convicted murderer, had read about the shooting of the banded bird in Louisiana and both of them were eager to learn more about the man who had banded them. "Little did I think when I stamped that verse on the tag that little duck carried away, that the message would ever find its way into a prison cell, and lodge in the heart of a murderer."

Beyond the tremendous publicity and the overwhelming response, Jack's inspired banding system had an important

A full view of Jack's goose trap (ca. 1924). *The long sides were swung out of the way and secured. Barley was spread inside the trap to lure the skittish birds.*
(Dr. R.D. Sloane)

practical side and ultimately affected the most important piece of legislation for migratory birds, up to that time.

By 1915 the Migratory Bird Act of 1913 was in need of further revision. The constitutionality of the law was being questioned as many states insisted that they, and not the federal government, were responsible for the regulation of hunting practices. Congressional aides who were versed in constitutional matters concurred with the states' contention. Any challenge to the act would ultimately be ruled in favour of the states. However, these experts offered a solution: If this law was ever transformed into a treaty between the United States and Canada, this constitutional concern would be swept aside because treaties overruled any state matters. Besides, many argued that legislation affecting migratory birds would obviously be better served if it were invoked in both countries that were involved in the migration.

With that in mind, Henry Ford and other interested parties began to push for the ratification of a treaty between the United States and Canada (represented diplomatically by Great Britain). One of the major proponents in the United States was William Hornaday, the notorious bad boy of the conservation movement and first director of the world-famous Bronx Zoo. Although he was castigated for his inflated ego and overbearing demeanour, few questioned his ability to move conservationists' mountains.

> Hornaday's concern for the preservation of endangered wild creatures, and his notable lack of concern for the feelings of those who did not agree with him, brought him fame (and a measure of success) far beyond that of most of the other conservationists of his time. But militants seldom attract eulogists. The directness with which he attacked every problem accounts for the planned obscurity into which other conservationists let his name drop immediately after his death.

Frank Graham's comments in *Man's Dominion: The Story of Conservation in America* notwithstanding, Jack Miner became a good friend of this iconoclast. Through Henry Ford's interest in the creation of the Migratory Bird Treaty, Jack and Hornaday became allies in the conservation movement; their alliance remained strong right up to Hornaday's death in 1937.

As part of the campaign to ratify the treaty, Manly Miner, acting as his father's secretary, diligently began writing out the duck- and goose-banding records to date, and he forwarded a copy to Hornaday. Another copy was sent to Robert Borden, the Canadian Prime Minister, in Ottawa. Jack Miner's banding records were taken seriously because at that time there was little concrete evidence as to the migratory habits of these birds.

Though he was by no means the originator of bird banding (the early Romans had marked birds), Jack was a pioneer in the "scientific" investigation of birds' habits. Professor C. C. Mortonsen of Denmark was considered the founder of systematic bird banding. In 1899 he began tagging and monitoring the travels of storks and starlings. In the United States, Dr. Leon Coles and Mr. Howard Cleaves were the earliest practitioners; their work began shortly after the turn of the century. In 1905 Percy Taverner began banding in Canada. While Jack started banding four years later, his subjects (particularly Canada geese) were unique. One periodical made this comment about Jack's work: "Not only has the information received from the tagging of these birds given Jack Miner knowledge as to the whereabouts of the birds, but the facts regarding their migration have never been obtained by any other man on the continent . . ."

Through the untiring efforts of men like Hornaday in the United States and Gordon Hewitt, Consulting Zoologist to the Dominion government ("the most energetic and effective advocate of wildlife preservation within the Canadian civil service"), the international treaty was agreed to in principle. Hornaday acknowledged Jack's contribution in a letter to him: "All this could not have been carried out had it not been for your duck-banding records between 1905 and 1915."

The Migratory Bird Treaty was ratified by Canadian Parliament (as the Canadian Migratory Birds Convention Act) in 1917. In the United States, President Woodrow Wilson signed the Migratory Bird Treaty Act into law on July 3, 1918. Janet Foster in *Working for Wildlife* suggests: "The Migratory Bird Treaty was much more than an important step. As a continental protection policy designed for continental travellers, its significance and value are as important today as in 1916, perhaps even more so, for North America is the only continent in the world whose bird populations are covered by an international agreement of such magnitude."

James B. Trefethen in his book, *An American Crusade for Wildlife*, gave this summary of the precedent-setting treaty:

Under regulations promulgated by the Secretary of Agriculture through the Bureau of Biological Survey and their Canadian

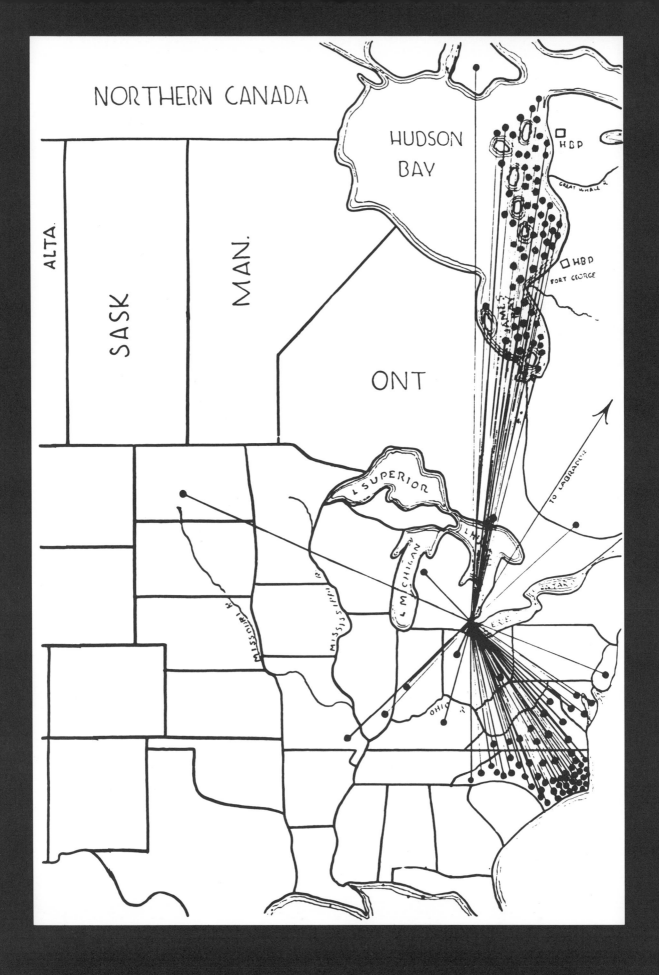

counterparts, most of the destructive abuses of the migratory-bird exploitation were eliminated. The sale of game birds covered by the Treaty was prohibited at all times, spring shooting and night shooting were abolished, and the plume birds and those classified as song and insectivorous species were accorded full legal protection. Daily bag limits—extremely generous by modern standards but still drastic by the standards of the time—were imposed on all migratory birds classified as game . . . In recognition of their threatened status, closed seasons were imposed on the hunting of wood ducks, swans and all species of shore birds except snipe and woodcock; shooting sandpipers, plovers, yellowlegs, and the other shorebirds had been a traditional spring sport for a century or more. Hunters were restricted to the use of shotguns of ten-gauge or less, effectively eliminating the huge puntguns that had been instruments of mass slaughter in the hands of market gunners.

Although, naturally, there were dissenters, the new treaty gained the support of those who mattered most: the sportsmen associations and the gun manufacturers. They realized that hunting would continue as a popular pastime only if it was carefully regulated. The provinces and states were allowed some autonomy; they could pass their own legislation for specific situations but, on the whole, they fell in line with their federal counterparts. For the first time a sense of coherence was seeping into the highly decentralized, albeit new, field of wildlife management.

Amidst this eruption of consciousness-raising, Jack received some good news from the Ontario government. Following pressure put upon it by members of the Essex County Game Protective Association and other interested parties, the provincial government, in 1917, declared Jack's home a crown game preserve, the first of its kind in the province. The hunting of migrating fowl was abolished within a one-mile radius of the sanctuary, and Jack received a small yearly grant.

Unfortunately, the Canadian federal government's role in wildlife conservation reached its zenith shortly after World War I, with the Commission of Conservation's Wildlife Conference in 1919. The Commission had been established ten years earlier by the Dominion government and, according to Janet Foster: "The Commission was unique, intended to be an independent, autonomous, objective, and fully non-partisan body that would explore all questions pertaining to natural resource conservation in Canada. To ensure its non-partisan nature, the Commission was established not as a part of usual government machinery for which the party in power is politically responsible, but as a body responsible only to Parliament as a whole."

However, she comments later on: "The Commission was given no executive or administrative powers; its function was purely advisory, its duty to collect and disseminate information on natural resources and make recommendations to Parliament for their more efficient development and conservation."

Opposite: The locations of hunters who acknowledged shooting Jack's banded birds were marked on maps. This one charts these locations as of 1924. Jack used these maps to demonstrate the migratory flight paths of the birds.
(Miner Collection)

Naturally, the Commission was heavily criticized during its lifetime. Some charged that the body overlapped much of the work done by other departments. Parliamentarians argued that an independent body, responsible only to Parliament, was inconsistent with the Canadian system of government. And, of course, there were those who criticized the government expenditures for the Commission, even though it was a relatively small outlay.

Nevertheless, Foster contends that the Commission played a useful role.

The Commission made its most notable contribution in the field of wildlife preservation. Once the migratory bird protec-

In these two photos (ca. 1922) Ted (left), Jack, and Jasper dump corn into a punt, then Jasper shovels corn onto the bank as Jack provides the power. By this time, about 15,000 bushels of corn were being consumed each year.
(Ford Motion Pictures, Miner Collection)

tion issue came before government in 1913, the Commission took up the wildlife cause, advocating protection not just for migratory birds but for all endangered bird and mammal species. Government members and American representatatives were frequently invited to address the annual meetings on all aspects of wildlife preservation, and each year valuable recommendations for greater wildlife protection were invariably found among the Commission resolutions. The Commission took much more than a passing interest in the establishment of parks and sanctuaries [the first bird refuges since 1887 were established on Bonaventure Island and Perce Rock, Quebec in 1918].

The Commission of Conservation's Wildlife Conference convened on February 18, 1919, and lasted two days. Attending the gathering were federal and provincial officials in charge of wildlife administration, local game organizations (including Jack's group in Essex County) and special representatives of the American wildlife movement: John Burnham, President of the American Game Protective Association and a major participant in the Migratory Bird Treaty negotiations; William Hornaday; and Edward Nelson, Chief of the United States Biological Survey.

Numerous papers were presented during the conference and, according to Foster's research, "The sanctuary idea sparked a great deal of interest among the delegates." As one of the pioneers in the sanctuary movement, Jack was allowed to address the participants. He outlined his humble beginning, pointed out the religious nature of his philosophy, and explained his arduous, though successful attempt to create his sanctuary. In effect, this conference officially introduced Jack Miner as a leading figure within the conservation movement.

The conference was adjourned with spirits high and recommendations for wildlife conventions to be held annually. Unfortunately, the euphoria was short-lived and never again was such an open conference held. There were two obvious factors for this policy reversal. First of all, Gordon Hewitt, the prime mover of the conservation movement within the Canadian government, died tragically in 1920 at the age of thirty-six. Secondly, the Commission of Conservation was abolished by Prime Minister's Arthur Meighen's government in 1921. Meighen had long been one of the body's staunchest critics.

In 1922 a Dominion-provincial wildlife conference was held but it was a closed-door session with no outside organizations invited. Janet Foster notes that this conference "marked the final acceptance by the federal government of its responsibilities in the field of wildlife preservation." While it was certainly a victory for the cause, Foster cautions that it did not result in an overwhelming change in government policymaking.

> . . . it was to be many more years before well-planned, well-funded government programs for wildlife conservation were to be developed. Public awareness of the importance of wildlife and a growing concern for the environment was also to take

many more years to develop [this is a debatable point for the millions who heard Jack Miner lecture]. In this respect, Americans were far ahead of Canadians. Both the conservation and preservation movements began in the United States at the turn of the century and since then American naturalists, conservationists, scientists, politicians, and concerned citizens have willingly taken up the cause. Part of the reason is that America's natural environment changed far more rapidly and to a far greater degree than Canada's.

Seemingly, as the euphoria surrounding wildlife conservation was fading in Canada, Jack Miner's star was rising and for the remainder of his life he was recognized as one of the greatest conservationists in the world, a man in tune with the natural world. Jack demonstrated his magic touch once more during the early years of the Roaring Twenties.

One of the largest and most majestic of all migrating birds, the whistler swan, was threatened with extinction, but this time man wasn't the culprit. Another majestic natural wonder was the source of the problem: Niagara Falls. It seemed that the warm spring weather of North Carolina was inducing the swans to abandon their winter homes in late March. However, the long, often brutal Canadian winter had not yet broken and migrating whistlers could find little open water upon which to alight. The Niagara River offered the only haven for the birds since the swift current kept the water open year round. Unfortunately, these were perilous waters, as Manly explains: "The water is warmer than the ice and as the ice floes would come to this water it would form a fog in the air and the swans would alight in this open water and as they drifted down the river toward the falls the fog would increase so birds or humans could not see the falls."

Hundreds of innocent slumbering birds were swept over the cliffs each spring. Most were killed instantly as they smashed upon the rocks below. Others, stunned by the plunge, floated head down and eventually drowned. Miraculously, a few managed to survive and they usually ended up on the ice bridge that formed over the river below the falls. However, this was a short-lived haven, for most of these survivors eventually died on the ice because of the injuries they sustained or the trauma of the entire episode.

William "Red" Hill of Niagara Falls, Ontario, one of Niagara's daredevils (he had gone over the falls, too, in a barrel) had often witnessed this savage rite of spring. Over the years he had also seen hundreds of ducks and geese suffer this same fate. However, Hill observed that, since the establishment of the Jack Miner Sanctuary, wild geese had not been seen near Niagara Falls. Yet the swans were still coming and many were needlessly dying. Hill often braved the trek across the ice bridge to rescue the injured swans (the rescue attempt was even more dangerous considering the fact that, in a bureaucratic stroke of genius, rescuing these birds was an illegal act).

Jack had been apprised of the whistler swan tragedy and, from longtime residents of the Niagara area, he learned that this had been the fate of many Canada geese until recently. Jack saw the obvious solution: "If I could get some whistling swans as decoys, perhaps the swans would come to the other end of the lake the same as the geese." In 1923 Jack arranged with Red Hill and government officials for the capture of six surviving swans and they were shipped to his sanctuary. Jack tended their wounds and diligently enlarged his ponds for his expected guests. The next spring the town of Kingsville witnessed a string of 1,500 whistler swans flying overhead. The birds circled over Jack's sanctuary and turned south, eventually landing in the open water of Lake Erie some two miles away. The peaceful voyagers were greeted by a bombardment as many overanxious and unlawful hunters opened fire upon them.

This drawing (ca. 1922) portrays Red Hill's dramatic rescue of an injured whistler swan after its plunge over Niagara Falls. (Miner Collection)

Jack poses for granddaughter Wilhelmina with two of the swans provided by Red Hill (ca. 1934). (Paul Lundstedt)

Two Mounties were sent to patrol the shore and protect the swans, day and night, during their stop-over. Word of this majestic gathering spread across the continent and visitors poured into the tiny community to witness the spectacle. The crowd on one Sunday was estimated to be about 15,000 and newspapers got caught up in the excitement, too. The Jack Miner legend was growing. According to one account:

> But thousands [of swans] have come to the bay and bar in the lake where Geese gather, and fewer and fewer are seen about Niagara, so that it would appear that they have found out about the bird sanctuary and have changed the whole course of migration from the eastern end. At any rate, none have gone over the falls in two years.
> Strangely enough, wild rice upon which Swans feed in their winter quarters in the Carolinas has sprung up and formed a wild marsh in the little bay, and where swans may gather in the Fall and feel quite safe. Jack refuses to talk very much about this wild rice, but some wise folk think he knows how it got its start.

The whistler swans proved to be much more skittish than Canada geese, and their annual stop-over brought them only as close to the sanctuary as the shore of Lake Erie. However, the geese were not as reluctant and the number of arrivals each spring was well into the thousands. Many more geese were visiting each fall, too. It now took over 14,000 bushels of corn to feed the weary, ravenous guests, for there were few spots along the way where they could calmly feed and rest. Naturally, as the number of geese increased, so did Jack's success at banding them.

The returning tags revealed that the birds were travelling along two distinct routes, one close to the Atlantic coast (now called the Atlantic Flyway) and another near the middle of the continent (the Mississippi Flyway). However, Jack had re-shaped these ancient skyways—something no one had done before. Wildlife author H. Albert Hochbaum in *Travels and Traditions of Waterfowl* notes: "Faithful as they are to their home range, however, geese are elastic in their use of migration routes and wintering quarters. Jack Miner's sanctuary, in southern Ontario, gives the history of a new goose tradition, the birds being few in the beginning and increasing in the lifetime of one man to many thousands more."

The significance of Jack's work did not go unnoticed by the scientific community. In 1921, in homage to his banding prowess, Dr. Frederick Lincoln of the U.S. Biological Survey visited Jack in an effort to learn more about his successful bird-banding technique. According to Manly, "Dr. Lincoln came to live with father and mother three springs in succession for from three to five days to help father band birds and making drawings of our nets, traps, etc.—traps father had to invent and rebuild twenty times to get them perfect." Lincoln's visit was not merely a goodwill gesture, for there was indeed a paucity of scientific data vis-à-vis waterfowl. Seven years following his first visit, the Biological Survey was still lacking the proper information as important legislation affecting wildlife preserva-tion was on the legislative agenda. According to Trefethen: "One of the admitted weaknesses in the camp of the propo-nents of the wildlife refuge bills before Congress was a dearth of scientific information on the status and movements of the various segments of the continental waterfowl population."

In the meantime, as a part of his conservation crusade, Jack Miner had personally orchestrated the development of many privately supported wildlife sanctuaries. By the mid-'20s his pleas for more "self-serve cafeterias" were paying dividends. Among those who had begun sanctuaries were E. E. Dupont of Maryland, Judge Arthur J. Tuttle and Henry B. Joy (foun-der of the Packard Motor Company) in Detroit, and F. D. Bailey of Oklahoma. Some influential Detroiters were so caught up in the sanctuary "craze" that the Detroit Board of Commerce formulated a plan to establish a bird sanctuary on Isle Royale, a scenic island located far away in Lake Superior. In 1924 Jack was the special guest and advisor to the board as more than 100 members chartered the Canadian steamer *Noronic* and cruised up to the isolated northern island. Upon visiting the island and discovering rarities like the wood cari-bou (the most southerly of the breed), Jack recommended that the entire island be declared a refuge. Today it is one of Amer-ica's national parks.

Jack's crusading was not limited to the United States; many sanctuaries were created in Canada as well. Some were established by the provincial governments—in Nova Scotia and Manitoba, for example. Others were realized solely through the efforts of private individuals. A Calgary newspaper in 1929 featured the bird sanctuary belonging to George Pickering, "Alberta's Jack Miner." However, Jack's efforts to create more sanctuaries were focussed primarily upon the United States. The birds required more areas of safety during their Southern swing, for Jack's bands revealed a dramatic trend in the number of birds killed. While American hunters were wont to criticize Canadians for the decline in the game bird population, Jack felt otherwise. "The United States has more hunters than Canada has population. . . . Can you blame me for being a little irritated at some of us Yankees condemning us Canadians for the scarcity of ducks and geese? Especially when you consider the fact that I have more goose tags returned from one Southern state [North Carolina] than I have from the whole of Canada, including Eskimo territory." North Carolina was given considerable attention and Jack was instrumental in creating sanctuaries there.

Jack (in the foreground) with members of the Detroit Board of Commerce on board the Noronic as they cruise up to Isle Royale in 1924.
(Miner Collection)

Jack also worked very closely with the Izaak Walton League in the United States. This nation-wide organization, named for the legendary British angler, was deeply committed to the preservation of wildlife resources, particularly in light of the new threat to the waterfowl population. Trefethen notes:

> But to men who possessed a degree of foresight, dark clouds were visible on the horizon. Under the pressures of a growing population and an expanding economy, waterfowl habitat was shrinking. Along the Mississippi and its far-flung tributaries, swamps and marshes were being drained behind a growing system of levees; and burgeoning towns and cities were spewing their wastes into once-pure waters. Back from the rivers, increasingly intensive agriculture was encroaching upon the prime, waterfowl-breeding habitat of the Great Plains.

For all the efforts of Jack and other proponents of sanctuaries, Trefethen pointed out: "If waterfowl were to be saved in any numbers the choicer wetlands had to be preserved through public ownership, not only in the breeding grounds of the North but in wintering areas of the South with protected resting places in between."

In 1929, during Herbert Hoover's presidency (Hoover was the most famous, not to mention the most influential, member of the Izaak Walton League), Senator Peter Norbeck of South Dakota and Congressman August H. Andressen of Minnesota introduced a bill that was eventually enacted as the Migratory Bird Conservation Act. The new law enabled federal authorities to purchase the valuable wetlands for refuges and set in motion the development of wildlife sanctuaries. With reference to Jack Miner's leadership, the Hamilton *Herald* noted that "so successful is Jack's sanctuary idea that in 1929 the United States copied his example to the extent of voting eight million dollars to be spent in their country building such sanctuaries in every state of the United States."

As a tribute to his dedication Jack, in 1929, was awarded the Outdoor Life Gold Medal by the prestigious Outdoor Writers Association of America. The citation acknowledged Jack as the "father of the waterfowl refuge area" and it added that Jack "has done more than any other person to encourage the establishment of sanctuaries where migratory fowl may rest and breed." Jack was the first Canadian to receive the award and it was one of countless honours and tributes he received throughout the last twenty-five years of his life.

The significance of Jack's effort was cruelly magnified that same year, with the onset of a severe drought that dried up the marshlands in North America and threatened the survival of waterfowl. The severity of the drought did not go unnoticed during the early years of Franklin Roosevelt's presidency. In one of his many startling policy measures he appointed Jay N. "Ding" Darling, a famous political cartoonist of all things, as the chief of the Bureau of Biological Survey. However,

Trefethen observed that "Darling brought to the bureau an enthusiasm and vigor that had not been seen in years. And, although few were aware of the fact, the new bureau chief also had been a Phi Beta Kappa biology major at Beloit College." Darling petitioned every major wildlife conservation group (including all the Izaak Walton League chapters) and asked for their support of and recommendations for the national refuge program. Jack Miner's opinions were made known during this period of inquiry, and when President Roosevelt directed the first one million dollars to be provided for the purchase and rental of lands as refuge for migratory birds and other wildlife, the Toronto *Globe* gave Jack his due, for he had "given leadership and a sense of direction to conservation." Eventually a total of six million dollars was diverted to Darling's bureau for "Uncle Sam's duck puddles."

Jack's exploits did not escape the attention of writers or cartoonists. This cartoon appeared in many publications during the 1920s.
(Miner Collection)

Darling's theories of wildlife conservation were very similar to Jack's and, in 1935, he introduced sweeping changes to hunting regulations—something that had been a point of contention for Jack ever since the acceptance of the Migratory Bird Treaty (he dubbed it the Unfinished Migratory Bird Treaty).

With regard to the length of the hunting season Jack wrote: "At the present time [1929] the Treaty allows any state or province three and a half months' open season, which is unjust to the Canadian sportsmen and the sportsmen of the Northern United States. My tagging system has proven that ducks and geese are in the southern states only three or four months of the year, and three and a half of these months are open season—which is wrong."

The daily bag limit (twenty-five a day for ducks) had also concerned Jack. He and William Hornaday were two of the more boisterous critics of this article within the Treaty. While some states had taken the initiative and reduced the bag limits, most of the vital Southern states adhered to the overly generous Treaty bag limits. Jack argued: "Now I am convinced that a bag limit as a law is a failure, as it cannot be enforced. Its only motive and advantages are to educate the people that slaughter is unsportsmanlike, but what kind of education is this—a lawful privilege for any individual to shoot 2,500 ducks and 800 geese in one season."

Darling's new regulations dealt with many of Jack's concerns. The open season was slashed to thirty days; bag limits were reduced to ten ducks and four geese a day; the use of bait (like corn) or live decoys to lure the birds (also two of Jack's big concerns) were outlawed; and shotguns capable of holding more than three shots at a loading were ruled illegal. Again, the press played up Jack's role in this significant change in hunting regulations; one article explaining the new law was entitled "Jack Miner Wins."

While Jack was an acclaimed shaper of government policy, rarely did he actually take part in wildlife conservation activities from the "other side"—that is, as a member of government-appointed committees. Indeed, Jack's appearances in these official capacities were often comically disastrous. In 1931 he was appointed to the Ontario government's special commission of inquiry into wild game problems (studying the decline of the game population). The committee toured the province and heard from thousands of people from all manner of villages, towns, and cities. Invariably, these meetings would turn into a Jack Miner appreciation night. People were more interested in hearing from Jack than airing their own views. Local newspapers, too, would focus more upon a Jack Miner personal appearance than the underlying rationale for his presence. Jack was more effective as a "lone wolf," guided by his own set of principles. He was never much of a manager and, fortunately, he never had to be—his family looked after that department.

Jack never stopped tinkering, even as he approached his seventieth birthday. It was simply foreign to his nature to be idle. In 1934 he arranged for twenty-four specially banded geese to be shipped to Manitoba. The purpose of the shipment was scientific in nature: Jack wanted to see if the geese would follow the local western migration route instead of the familiar Mississippi or Atlantic Flyways. The study showed that, indeed, the geese somehow relocated their traditional route; as early as the winter of 1935 one of the experimental geese was reportedly killed in North Carolina.

Jack turned his attention to the plight of the wood duck, recognized as an endangered species as far back as 1917. Utilizing the old tried and true method of using hens on ducks as "stepmothers," he was able to hatch up to 500 wood ducks a year. Reports from 1938 noted that these spectacularly beautiful birds were flying around the sanctuary "like pigeons." He also began the practice of banding teal, a small variety of duck noted for its long-range migration to the Caribbean. Naturally, his famous bands brought him even more recognition as Caribbean islanders began shooting down his winged missionaries.

Some of his friends and supporters attempted to have him knighted by the King for his lifelong devotion to the "cause," but the practice of knighting non-Britishers had been abandoned following World War I. Nevertheless, Jack's exploits were recognized by the Crown: Jack Miner's name was included upon King George VI's 1943 birthday list as a recipient of the Order of the British Empire. The rationale for the award was simple and to the point: "For the greatest achievement in Conservation in the British Empire."

The Sanctuary Today

*In the still of an autumn
morning the spirit of Jack
Miner is a tangible presence
on the sanctuary grounds.*

◀ *A mated pair of Canada
geese soar over the Jack
Miner Bird Sanctuary in the
dawn light of October.*

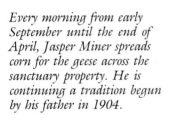

Every morning from early September until the end of April, Jasper Miner spreads corn for the geese across the sanctuary property. He is continuing a tradition begun by his father in 1904.

The Miner sanctuary has long been one of Canada's major tourist attractions. In keeping with Jack's wishes, the grounds are open to the public year round with the exception of Sundays and there is no admission charge.

◄ During the migration season tens of thousands of wild geese find food and safety at the Miner home. Over the years equal numbers of nature lovers have come to witness the phenomenon.

◄ Each Saturday in November Jasper Miner and his helpers band between 400 and 500 newly captured ducks and geese. Each band carries the message, "Write Jack Miner, Kingsville, Ontario," and a simple Bible verse. Since 1915 over 80,000 migrating waterfowl have been similarly ordained as "Missionaries of the Air."

From his office overlooking the birds Manly Miner conducts the business management of the sanctuary. It is a job he has been doing since he was just thirteen years of age.

*Since Jack's death in 1944,
Manly and Jasper Miner have
devoted themselves to preserving their father's legacy. They
invite one and all to visit
their home and share the
wonder of the wild geese.*

. . . during the last fifteen years I have been lecturing, I have no doubt spoken to a million or more school children in North America, where I emphasize to them and encourage them to build a birdhouse. If I can get a child to build a birdhouse he becomes a conservationist.

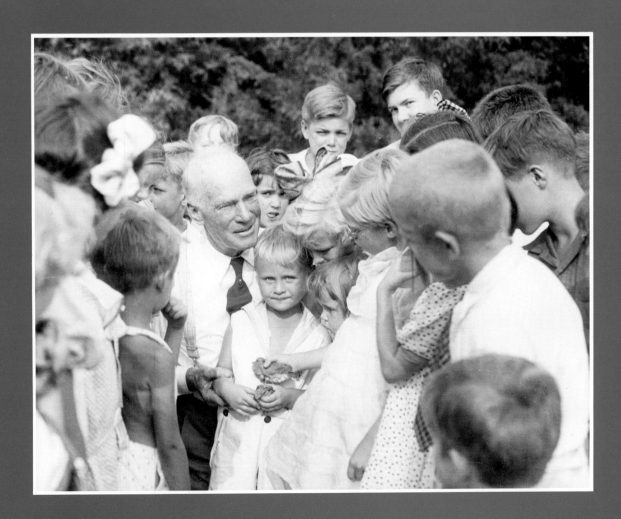

5

An Educational Conservation Campaign

THERE have been many notable contributors to the history of the conservation movement in North America. Henry Clepper, Chairman of the Editorial Committee of the Natural Resources Council of America, notes that: "Of the thousands of men and women who contributed to the advancement of knowledge about resources and to their management in the public interest [in the United States], a few hundred stand out."

In introducing his book of biographies of these few hundred, Clepper singles out some of these individuals for special mention: Theodore Roosevelt as the "pioneer statesmen" in resource conservation; Gifford Pinchot as a national leader in forest management; Aldo Leopold as an innovator in wildlife management; and John Muir for his efforts in park and wilderness preservation (and as founder of the Sierra Club). Similarly for Canada, Janet Foster identifies a handful of such "far-sighted, resourceful, dedicated" individuals (who in the Canadian system all happened to be civil servants). It was these men who took their own interests and concerns about wildlife preservation and helped to mould them into government policy. Included in this group were Howard Douglas, Superintendent of Rocky Mountain Parks; Robert Campbell, Director of the Forestry Branch of the Department of the Interior; James B. Harkin, Commissioner of Dominion Parks; Maxwell Graham, "self-appointed Chief of the parks' three-man 'Animal Division' "; and Gordon Hewitt, Dominion Entomologist with the Department of Agriculture and Consulting Zoologist to the Dominion government.

Many of these notable individuals in both Canada and the United States carried on their battle for resource conservation in the back rooms and corridors of power, far from the view of the general public. Their main concern was to effect changes in conservation-related legislation and practices, not in popular attitudes and opinions about such matters. But there were some who attempted to alert the public to the danger that lay in store if man's wasteful practices were not checked, and

Overleaf: Jack surrounded by a group of children as he lets them hold some small birds at the sanctuary (ca. 1927).
(Miner Collection)

Jack holds a Canada goose during one of his radio broadcasts in the 1930s.
(Dr. R.D. Sloane)

others who were more zealous in sharing their ideas and viewpoints. Conservation historian James Trefethen notes, for example, that Clinton Merriam used his offices to publish and disseminate information to the general public about the benefits of protecting birds; that Dr. William T. Hornaday's prolific writings received wide circulation and acceptance; and that Gifford Pinchot's leadership of U. S. forest resource management was "almost evangelical."

Such efforts at publicizing the cause of conservation and winning converts had their beneficial effects and are most laudable. But they pale in comparison to the activities of Jack Miner, which included extensive lecturing, numerous writings, and radio broadcasts, all in behalf of wildlife preservation. In the early part of the twentieth century, an editorial in the Minneapolis *Journal* proclaimed Jack "the Father of the Conservation Movement on the continent." It was a title to which he would re-establish the right each year for almost forty years after his very first attempt to attract wild geese to his sanctuary in 1904.

By luring the geese to his ponds in 1908, Jack had altered a migration pattern that had been unchanged in living memory. This fact alone gained him attention. But by starting the practice of banding ducks in 1909 and following it up with the banding of Canada geese in 1915, Jack gained further prominence and recognition as hunters returned the tags and newspapers ran stories about it. Through a news syndication service, as many as a thousand newspapers would pick up the story of the killing of a duck or goose bearing a Miner tag. This coverage increased even more when he struck upon the idea of stamping Bible verses on the bands, making his ducks and geese missionaries of the air.

The first such banded goose was shot by a Southern sportsman who proudly displayed his kill to his assembled friends on a downtown street corner. They all curiously examined the inside of the tag on one of its legs and Jack later wrote about the aftermath of that investigation:

> . . . nestled away on the inside of the tag, was deeply stamped the following four words, "Have faith in God." One who was present wrote me that when those last four words were read, all voices seemed hushed; for they had the effect of a real benediction on that street corner.
>
> There were, undoubtedly, newspaper reporters present when the so-called "benediction" was read. In less than one week, this one wild goose tag brought to my country mail-box nearly fifty enquiring letters. Some were very lengthy ones. But the great majority of them were ones enquiring, "What is your religion? What is your religion?"

Jack reported that his mail more than doubled after he began stamping Scripture messages on the bird bands.

People's interest in and curiosity about Jack's sanctuary had been piqued several years earlier. Local residents and visitors from as far away as Detroit had begun visiting Jack's home shortly after the geese had first started to arrive on their semi-annual migrations. As new reports and word-of-mouth spread the story of Jack's "miracle," the number of visitors to the

Canada geese arising from the back ponds of the Miner sanctuary as viewed by a visitor from Jack's "Oblookatory", a viewing area on the second floor of the family carriage house (ca. 1924). By having Canada geese stop at his home, Jack Miner altered a migration pattern that had remained unchanged in living memory.
(Ford Motion Pictures, Miner Collection)

sanctuary increased dramatically. And people were not satisfied with just reading about Jack's feats, nor even with observing them in practice at his home; they wanted to see Jack "in the flesh" and hear in his own words the "why's" and "wherefore's" of his activities and beliefs. In 1910, to satisfy the public interest, to broaden people's understanding of and involvement in conservation, and to earn some additional income to offset the burgeoning costs of feeding the steadily growing number of geese, Jack embarked on a lecturing career that would span the next thirty years. While the first few years were spent talking mainly to groups and organizations in the local area, he would eventually travel the length and breadth of Canada and the United States, speaking to everyone from simple schoolchildren to the President of the United States and the Prime Minister of Canada.

In 1915 Jack's good friend, Henry Ford, sent over a cameraman from his Highland Park motion picture laboratory to make a film of the sanctuary for Jack to use during his speaking engagements. Ford, an early proponent of the use of motion pictures for publicity and educational purposes, recognized that movies of Jack's activities around the sanctuary grounds would heighten the impact of his already engaging presentations. Jack greatly appreciated Ford's gesture, and in thanking him told him on several occasions ". . . to just have my speech or lecture without the movies to follow my remarks was like bread without butter."

Every few years from 1915 on, Ed Flickenger would visit the Miner home to update the films. On tour, Jack would first lecture unaided on conservation and other topics for about an hour to an hour and a half, and then provide a running commentary during the projection of the half-hour film and some hand-tinted slides, often injecting a humorous story or aside and occasionally breaking into song.

Jack's lecturing soon occupied a major portion of the time between the spring and fall migration periods. Scheduling became a demanding and time-consuming activity and was handled with consummate skill by his eldest son. Manly Miner looked after all the details of the trips, but remained at home to manage the business affairs of both the sanctuary and the brickyard. From there he plotted publicity and promotional campaigns for Jack's lectures with a shrewdness and originality on a par with any such public relations efforts undertaken at the time. Inquiries about speaking engagements swelled to hundreds and then thousands each year. By 1926 he was receiving a thousand requests annually from the United States and Canada, and even the occasional one from England and Scotland. (At the time of his death in 1944 he left behind some 4,000 invitations he had been unable to accept.)

To facilitate the handling of so many invitations and requests, a standard information sheet was formulated and sent out to prospective sponsors. A sample of a 1923 mailing gives a flavour of Jack's humour, his down-to-earth approach, and his self-proclaimed "A,B,C education":

Dear Friend:

For those who are interested in my lecture, to save time and avoid misunderstanding, I submit this brief explanation;

1. My evening lecture takes about two hours, therefore no other program is really necessary. My afternoon lecture for children is usually put on at four or four-fifteen and takes about one hour. The usual admission fee is ten cents for children, with teachers free; for evening meetings, 35 and 50 cents.

2. I have about forty slides and two thousand feet of motion picture film, but have no machine to show either—you supply the machine. The slides and films are both standard size. Pathescope machines will not show my pictures. MACHINE MUST BE standard size.

3. My lectures are all based on facts gathered from personal

Opposite: A typical handbill for a lecture appearance by Jack. (Miner Collection)

Jack prepares to board a train at a stop on one of his many long and arduous lecture tours (ca. 1932).
(Miner Collection)

To-Night !

"Jack Miner"

The Greatest Canadian Naturalist and Conservationist.

"The Man who made the Wild Goose Tame"

Victoria Opera House

Eight o'clock

It will prove one of the greatest educational and instructive speeches you have ever had the pleasure of listening to.

Motion picture of bird life which will astonish you, including the famous "crow trap" which captured 500 in one day.

Children's Matinee—10c.
Send your little ones to the Matinee at 4.15—you will NEVER regret it—they will NEVER forget it.

Reserved Seats, 50c.   **Rush, 25c.**

experience and observation, therefore, you are not getting a second-hand deal. As to my personality: I am just a grown up boy who was born bare-footed and raised on the toe of father's boot; now grown out of the pink into the silver-tip class, with all to be thankful for and nothing to boast of, as neither drouth nor freshet have affected my growth, and I am still carrying a hundred pounds of steam and no damper.

4. The money I get for my lectures all goes toward the upkeep of my bird sanctuary, and providing food for these God-given feathered creatures that pay no attention to boundary lines and belong to you as much as they do to me. Last spring (1922) I fed over two thousand bushels of ears of corn between February 20 and April 20.

5. In case you decide to have me come, please state most convenient way of getting in and out of your town and all being well I will be on hand like a sore thumb.

6. My charges in writing below. I pay my own expenses.

Jack Miner

The tours involved a highly orchestrated schedule and Jack kept up a hectic pace during them. In one tour during the first four months of 1927, for example, Jack made numerous appearances in eighteen towns and cities. Some of the locations included Minneapolis, Detroit, Toronto, Ottawa, Montreal, Chicago, several smaller towns and cities in Ontario, and a city in Iowa. During one stretch in February and March of that year, he spoke as many as five times a day for forty days in succession. A headline in the Toronto *Globe* captured the spirit of Jack's tour: "Jack Miner, the Napoleon of Conservation, launched a new campaign."

In later years Jack supplied his own motion picture projection equipment after he had been given the first portable 35-mm projector in Canada and had been supplied with safety film to avoid the technical and legal problems presented by the volatile nitrate film stock that was still then in general use. He would be accompanied by a travelling companion who would project the Ford motion pictures during Jack's lectures, and would act as a chauffeur when the tours were undertaken by automobile. At various times this role was carried out by sons Ted and Jasper and by Ercel Plant, the son of a brickyard employee.

Jack often talked to children at schools or in local auditoriums free of charge in the afternoons, urging them to have their parents bring them back to the admission-charge lecture in the evening. During one six-week period it was calculated that he spoke to over 200,000 schoolchildren. And while two lectures a day seems to have been the most common routine, it was not unusual for him to address as many as five or six groups in a day—and all but one of them free of charge.

Jack's efforts to bring conservation to the attention of one and all via his lectures are certainly impressive. They are even more impressive when one remembers that these tours were

undertaken during the later period of Jack's life, from ages forty-five to seventy-five. As some press reports pointed out, Jack's touring schedules were as hectic as a campaigning politician's—but the politician's only lasted for the duration of the campaign while Jack's lasted for thirty years. In one five-year period alone (1925–1930), Jack crossed Canada seven times. These lecture tours took him at various times from such wide-ranging locations as Alaska to Newfoundland, and from British Columbia to Florida. During his speaking career he appeared in many of the major meeting halls and auditoriums on the continent, including Carnegie Hall, the Ballroom of the Waldorf-Astoria, and Massey Hall.

His talks were sponsored by groups ranging all the way from major national organizations like the National Geographic Society, the American Camp Club, the American Game Protective Association, and the Izaak Walton League of America to local service clubs, churches and schools, and garden and flower clubs. He was as much at ease addressing heads of state, important industrialists, and university professors as he was speaking to the average working person and schoolchildren.

Some of his speaking engagements are particularly noteworthy. One was the trip to Winnipeg, Manitoba, in 1923 when Jack's paid lectures over a three-day period outdrew by 5,000 people former British Prime Minister David Lloyd George's

At a school in Kapuskasing, Ontario, in 1932, Jack enthralls another audience of schoolchildren. Family friend Colonel Fred K. Jasperson attests to his effect on children: "They would look up to him and their eyes would simply become absorbed. They were somewhere else."
(Miner Collection)

*Scenes from films shown by
Jack Miner on his tours.*
(Ford Motion Pictures, Miner Collection)

*Jack on stage preparing to
begin a lecture* (ca. 1926).

*Jack with robins trained to
come and eat from a tin dish
when he tapped on it with
a spoon* (ca. 1926).

*Jack and Jasper herd Canada
geese that have been caught
in his famous goose trap into
a holding pen where they
will be banded* (ca. 1923).

*Surrounded by roses in his
arbour at the sanctuary, Jack
waves good-by to the motion
picture camera* (ca. 1926).

free appearances for the same period. Manly Miner considers this episode one of the crowning glories of his promotional career:

> A week ahead I advised them [the sponsoring group] to have the Mayor meet the train and have a band out. They did all this plus having the Prime Minister of the Province, which resulted in the Press giving the occasion front page publicity.
>
> I had them schedule him to speak in two schools to children in the a.m. and two in the afternoon, and some service club at noon—no charges for those five appearances, but the chairman advised the children to bring their parents to the largest auditorium in the city which was some arena or football stadium as it was in the fall.

Another milestone in Jack's lecturing career was his selection as guest speaker for the National Convention of the Izaak Walton League at the Sherman Hotel in Chicago in 1927. Jack and his family were proud of the fact that on that occasion he shared the platform with U.S. Commerce Secretary Herbert Hoover, soon-to-be President of the United States, who was the League's special guest of honour.

Jack felt similarly flattered when in the following year he spoke in Ottawa at the Dominion United Church and was introduced by the Right Honourable Mackenzie King, Prime Minister of Canada, and dined with the Governor General, His Excellency Lord Willingdon. In his introduction Prime Minister King heaped praise on Jack and thanked him for his good works:

> I hardly think that [it] is necessary [to introduce him] as Mr. Miner is known to every audience in this great Canada of ours from Atlantic to Pacific, and not only in Canada but over the entire Continent. Mr. Miner is the one man whom we have to thank for having proved to us the regular habits of the migratory birds. We are glad to have him here because of himself, his interest in bird life and the great service that he has rendered to all classes in the world. We are also glad to have him here in order that we may express to him something of the debt which the people of Canada feel they owe him for the work he has done.

An additional engagement from which Jack received similar satisfaction was his last large speaking address, which took place in Chautauqua, New York, and had been arranged by Mrs. Thomas A. Edison, a close family friend. It was held at such a popular venue that speakers were booked into it two years in advance. A special added feature of this particular evening was music furnished by the Philadelphia Orchestra with Eugene Ormandy conducting.

No voice recording of any of Jack's full-fledged lectures are still in existence, and the only remaining complete transcript of any talks is that of an address to the fifty-ninth annual convention of the Ontario Education Association given at Convocation Hall in Toronto in April, 1920. Nevertheless, the form and content of his speeches have been captured in a narration of some of his motion picture films contained in the documentary film biography of Jack's life and times, *Wild Goose Jack*:

Here it is, ladies and gentlemen, my sanctuary in Kingsville. Now Kingsville is the most southerly town in the Dominion of Canada, and each spring and fall twenty thousand migrating honkers descend on my brickyard pond and help themselves to my self-serve cafeteria.

The Canada goose is one of the bravest and most intelligent creatures on earth—like my favourite gander, Jack Johnson here. He is a ferocious fighter who would defend the safety of his loved ones against any threat. The Canada goose is eternally loyal to its mate, setting a noble example for us to follow, and let me say a few words about loyalty—I believe every man has the right to take two women into his life, provided one of them is his mother-in-law!

My dear friends, we can have whatever we set our hearts on. I planted this forest, tree by tree, with the help of my boys. Everything I have done at my home is based on those words found in the book of Genesis: "Let man have dominion over all." These little beauties are bobwhite quail; this darling bird is one of the best friends a farmer ever had. Once grown, he will eat his weight in weed seeds and insects. I raise quail by the hundreds and let them loose throughout the country.

Oh, here we are, my pet robins with me in my rose arbour at the sanctuary. I got this idea from a young boy who wrote me that he'd managed to make a robin into a pet, and for some reason named him "Jack"—I guess because he had a crimson disposition too. Whenever I see these cheerful little robins I can't help but wish Canada geese were as friendly when I try to band those wily birds.

So how, you ask, do I take captive my winged messengers? Well, hovering over their unsuspecting heads is the most surefire, never-miss goose trap that God ever inspired man to create. Years of careful observation tell me when the time is exactly right to pull my trusty trip wire and take captive those innocent fowl. In a twinkling of an eye the commotion quiets down and I'm able to place a band bearing a verse of Scripture on each wild honker's leg, thus ordaining them "missionaries of the air."

Now I truly hope that each of you wonderful people comes to visit us—and please leave your wallets at home. There's no admission charge. Let my sanctuary be one place on earth where no money changes hands. You're all as welcome as the flowers in May. Thank you and good night.

Jack's appearance and stage manner caused some observers to describe a lecture by him as a combination vaudeville act,

Sunday school class, and nature lesson. His stature and rough-hewn look caused some people to describe him as a "genial bear" or to say he "looked like a lumberjack." But others saw him as a "youthful man of sixty-odd years, with a serene, unlined face, the heart of a boy, and the vision of a prophet." While a few thought he was not a talented speaker—possibly because he lacked the clear diction and polished grammar of the formally educated man—the vast majority were impressed with his abilities as an orator. One man even suggested that Jack would have been a great evangelist. Indeed, Governor Alfred Smith of New York in twice introducing Jack described him as "the Billy Sunday for the bird family," in reference to the then-popular evangelical preacher.

Jack's greatest talent seems to have been his ability to make his talk an intimate, virtually one-on-one experience for almost every member of the audience. Colonel Fred Jasperson, a prominent Kingsville citizen who knew Jack for many years, recalls that ability:

> I felt that Jack, when he spoke, was very sincere. He was telling you something he had experienced himself, and was drawing people into the picture he was trying to paint. He developed the picture in your own mind and I felt he was at one with everybody who was in the group. He made people feel that they were right in the drawing room with him and that he was telling them all the things that had happened.

What others have also described as Jack's "magnetic power over vast audiences," his highly appreciated sense of humour, his injection of "little local touches that bring him right into the hearts of his hearers," his "haunting wonderful voice"—and especially "his religious inspiration [which] came from his experience in his own humane touch with nature"—all these factors combined to make Jack's lecture an impressive and moving experience. A press report in the December 5, 1929, Lethbridge *Herald* conveys the impact that Jack's appearance had in that Alberta city:

> This famous man in his charming addresses Monday was humorist, optimist, naturalist, evangelist. He is an extraordinary character, natural, rough-hewn, almost primitive. Yet erstwhile fine and poetic and spiritual. At times he strikes a note of eloquence that bespeaks genius; again as did Lincoln he will spin stories of the frontier and wilderness with a smoothness and intimacy that fairly consumes his audience. And always there runs through his talks a sound philosophy, a philosophy that revolves around the existence of God as the great and loving Father not only of men, but of all His creations. There were moments at the service club luncheon when that large assemblage of business men were laughing hilariously; other moments when these same men held back tears as something of the pathos of life was touched with a sincerity, a delicacy, an understanding characteristic of this love of the wilderness.

It is little wonder, then, that one listener would summarize Jack's presentation as "a unique personality, a unique experience, a unique story told in a unique way. There's no other one in Jack's class." Quite clearly, those who attended his lectures felt the same way.

The growing publicity that Jack received as a result of his speaking appearances and touring only served to whet the public's interest in his work and ideas. Not only did Jack's mail increase and invitations for him to speak pour into the Miner home, but there was also a demand for him to share his experiences and philosophy with the public through the print and other mass media, which were then beginning to displace the spoken word as the primary methods of communication and persuasion. With the assistance and guidance of Manly, who understood the potential of such media, Jack embarked on a writing and broadcasting career.

Having had only three months of formal schooling and not having learned to read and write until he was thirty-five years old, Jack was at first a reluctant author. But Manly coaxed his father along:

> Between 1916 and 1922 I wrote father's stories as he would dictate them to me in spare time. In 1923 I published his book: "Jack Miner and the Birds: Some Things I Know About Nature". In the first nine months 4,000 copies were sold by direct mail, the profit being channelled into advertising of the book. The demand for the book grew, and I was soon selling it on a royalty basis of 20% instead of the usual 10%. Several editions of this book were published.

Jack wanted to produce a quality book at a relatively cheap retail price so that all his followers could read about his activities; and after interviewing several publishers Manly chose Ryerson Press in Canada. Soon the Miners were receiving requests for copies from people all over the world. On the basis of the book's success in Canada, Manly went to the United States and published a similar version with the Reilly Lee Publishing Company.

In addition to its popularity with readers, the book also enjoyed a measure of critical success. One reviewer wrote in the *Toronto Saturday Night* that *Jack Miner and the Birds* "is not only peculiarly authoritative but enfolds a romance the like of which I do not know for originality, intimacy and attractiveness among all that has been written about wild things." Another reviewer observed that "Jack Miner's story is told in a rich, forceful vernacular, marked by pithiness, wit and striking metaphor, mixed with homely philosophy" and that it was illustrated with "truly wonderful photographs." An admirer in the United States wrote in a letter to the editor of his local newspaper that the book was "the story of an ideal wrought into a working reality . . . an inspiration for all who would live more kindly and sanely in a world that still has too much of

Manly confers with Jack about some correspondence and discusses an idea for a future article (ca. 1930). (Dr. R.D. Sloane)

By 1930 Jack had become such a noted author and conservation authority that he was being used to sell subscriptions to Forest and Outdoors *Magazine.*
(Miner Collection)

The famous Jack Miner, a regular writer for "Forest and Outdoors"

"Grey Owl", Indian feature-writer of "Forest & Outdoors", whose articles have attracted international attention.

cruelty and destruction." And advertising for the book contained testimonials from such notables as Prime Minister Mackenzie King, Sir Adam Beck, William T. Hornaday of the New York Zoological Park, J. B. Harkin, and John B. Burnham, President of the American Game Protective Association.

As was often the case with Jack, publicity about his life and his work at the sanctuary increased rather than satisfied people's curiosity about the man and his beliefs. The public demand for another book conflicted with Jack's heavy schedule of work at the sanctuary and his lecture tours. Working with Manly, the publishers collected various newspaper articles that he and Jack had written, and compiled them into a book, *Jack Miner on Current Topics*, which was published in 1927. During Jack's lifetime several editions of the original *Jack Miner and the Birds* were published, but after his death in 1944 the two volumes were combined and published as a memorial edition under that same title.

Between the publication of these two books, Manly Miner began organizing a writing campaign that was characteristic of his systematic approach to publicity and promotion. The extensive press coverage of Jack's activities resulted in many requests for articles and his opinions on outdoor matters. Manly kept a file so that he knew the questions the public was asking, and proceeded to ghost-write articles with Jack on these popular topics. Getting these stories published posed no problem, according to Manly, and simply added to the spiralling publicity and attention:

> We never charged for these articles, but I had as high as thirteen articles appearing in one month's edition in thirteen different magazines or periodicals. So many did I have appearing from time to time that the largest magazines sent their writers or editors here for interviews which I arranged for in the summer when father was home and such periodicals as The Saturday Evening Post, The Colliers Weekly, The American Magazine, The American Weekly - Reader's Digest all carried feature articles which meant we were flooded with small publications and religious publications for articles [that they could publish themselves].

In addition to the serialization of *Jack Miner and the Birds* in the Toronto *Globe and Mail* in 1927, Jack published pieces in various newspapers across Canada and the United States on a wide range of topics: An article on interfering with nature appeared in the Edmonton *Journal* and the Victoria *Times* in 1926; a plea for a refuge system in the Detroit *Sunday Times* in 1927; a criticism of Ontario deer population control policy in the Stratford *Beacon* in 1928; an article "on himself" in the Detroit *Free Press* in 1928; and so on. Articles in magazines and periodicals were just as varied, dealing with topics such as pheasants in Canada, the menace of crows, his missionary geese, the "Unfinished Migratory Game Treaty," facts about

Manly arranged to have Jack's books published privately to ensure more control over their dissemination— not to mention earn higher-than-normal commissions.
(Miner Collection)

Jack works on his autobiography in a tent during one of his trips up north (ca. 1933).

(Dr. R.D. Sloane)

hawks, the hardship of being famous, and so forth. While the vast majority of these stories were printed in outdoor and sportsmen's magazines such as *Rod and Gun, Forest and Outdoors, Forest and Stream* and *Outdoor America*, others appeared in publications with quite different audiences, such as the Salvation Army's *The War Cry*. And while Manly most often preferred to remain behind the scenes, he, too, became a published author in his own right, helping to spread his father's ideas and continuing to do so after Jack died.

Then, in 1930, Jack began writing on a topic with which only he could deal. He was asked to contribute an article, "What my religion means to me," or "Why I believe there is a God," to a series that was to include contributions by Nellie McClung and Edgar Guest. But after he had completed it, his publishers suggested he hold off and use the article as a climax to his autobiography instead. After Manly had explained to his father what an "autobiography" was, Jack began work on his life story. Much of his time between 1930 and his death in 1944 was occupied by this soul-searching task. He spent long hours alone writing in the solitude of the woods during his trips north in the fall, and he had a dwarf-sized cabin in a rarely frequented area of the sanctuary grounds to which he would steal away to write during the rest of the year. After his death the manuscript remained locked up in a safe at home until 1969, when *Wild Goose Jack: Jack Miner, His Life and Religion* was published, sharing Jack Miner's story with the world again.

Jack's efforts to preach the message of conservation were not confined to merely books, magazines, and newspapers. Radio had emerged as a major new medium in North America in the 1920s. It had caught the imagination of the public and taken the continent by storm. By 1930 there were 13 million radio receivers in the United States, and in five years the number had risen to 30.5 million, which meant that almost every household in America contained a radio by 1935. Similar intense growth took place in Canada, with close to 600,000 radio-receiving-set licences being sold to receiver owners in 1931. Every evening millions of people huddled around their radio sets and attempted to hear their favourite programs through the crackles of interference that plagued reception in the early days. While most of the popular programs were of the entertainment or amusement type, people also listened to news and public affairs broadcasts, which kept them informed about the issues and personalities of the day. The voices that regularly emanated from the radio became well known and their owners were the first "stars" of broadcasting—although the "invisible" nature of the medium made them more anonymous than such stars are today.

Radio was born just as Jack was reaching the height of his career. His widespread reputation, the arresting quality of his voice, and his engaging, persuasive speaking style combined to make Jack a natural for this new medium of communication. His opportunity came in 1930 when Mr. Carl Nunn, President of the Halliday Lumber Company of Hamilton, Ontario, in conjunction with the Hamilton Bird Society, offered to sponsor a series of broadcasts by Jack. The series began on Tuesday, March 18, 1930, and ran for six consecutive Tuesdays on stations in Hamilton, London, and Toronto. The response was overwhelming. Between 5,000 and 6,000 letters of appreciation were received in the first two days following the broadcasts, and as many as 1,000 a day thereafter. All told, tens of thousands of letters and requests for information concerning the starting of bird clubs were received. Extra secretaries had to be brought in to answer all the mail, and one radio authority was quoted as saying Jack Miner was "the greatest drawing card a Canadian radio station ever had by many times."

The success of the series ensured a second one in 1931. The network carrying it was vastly expanded from the previous year with some seventy-eight participating stations, taking in every province in Canada and all the northern states in the United States. At least ten million people listened in to the first broadcast in the series, and the Hamilton Bird Society received 8,000 letters in the two days following it, with a total of 60,000 more pouring in as a result of the other six broadcasts. Jack was again heard on the Halliday program in 1932, and by 1934 the program was being carried on the Canadian Radio Commission chain (the forerunner of the Canadian Broadcasting Corporation). By this time Manly felt that his father's broadcasts could generate additional revenue to feed the geese, and unbeknownst to Jack he circulated a promotional letter offering ten half-hour broadcasts for 5,000 dollars. But nothing seems to have come as a result of this particular proposal.

Jack's prowess over the airwaves, however, did result in one particularly noteworthy radio-related honour. To mark the twenty-fifth anniversary of King George V's reign in 1935, a worldwide radio broadcast was held, with each Commonwealth

As Canada's representative in the Commonwealth-wide radio broadcast marking the silver anniversary of King George V's reign in 1935, Jack reads from a prepared text into a radio link-up in his home. (Dr. R.D. Sloane)

country participating. The Canadian Parliament selected Jack Miner to speak on behalf of Canada. Manly describes the circumstances surrounding the broadcast:

> Jack Miner's home was wired with two sets of wires so if one went bad they had another, and Canada's Prime Minister, The Honorable Mackenzie King sat in Ottawa as Master of Ceremonies and introduced Jack Miner who with my help had prepared a five minute address which Jack Miner delivered from his home in Kingsville. Jack Miner rehearsed his message and . . . he timed himself so that he finished five seconds before the end of the allotted time which brought him great praise from the radio operators and he personally received letters by the hundreds from sixty-five countries in the world.

In the two months following the broadcast Jack reportedly received over 8,000 letters, telegrams, and telephone messages from most parts of the British Empire and the United States.

After that zenith had been reached, Jack's radio career seems to have virtually ended. In 1936 he was a guest on a radio show hosted by his friend "Boss" Johnson on Station WLW in Cincinnati, which was part of an eighty-station NBC hook-up. And in 1943 Jack was the subject of a fifteen-minute nationally broadcast program in radio star Clare Wallace's series about renowned personalities. But by this time Jack was in his late seventies and had effectively retired from public life.

Jack's efforts to make conservation a living reality demonstrated that a single individual could do something for the benefit of God's creatures if he were committed enough and had sufficient will. And if his pronouncements had managed to leave any doubts about his sincerity or effectiveness, these were soon dispelled when visitors to the sanctuary watched Jack at work in his modern-day "garden of eden" where man lived in harmony with nature.

Even for someone as prominent as Henry Ford, a trip to

the sanctuary was an impressive and moving experience. America's leading industrialist had first read about Jack in a Detroit newspaper and talked about him and the sanctuary with an assembly-line employee who lived in Kingsville. Shortly after that conversation a trip had been arranged, and Jack describes the first of many warm visits to the Miner home:

> Yes, Mr. Ford first came here with a pair of high rubber boots, prepared, as he said, to "wade through a marsh and peek out at some wild geese"; when we walked among them with low shoes on, and even talked to them, that great man seemed spellbound. We have had many a good laugh about it since. He stood for a moment or two and looked; then, turning to me he said, "There are over three thousand of these Canadian honkers right here, in front of us; and I could throw a stone to the farthest one." Remember, friends, those birds weighed from ten to twelve pounds each; in other words, they were not domesticated canaries.

As Jack's fame grew in the 1920s, visitors often overran the carefully maintained grounds and gardens. Jack characterized the situation as one in which he "didn't get as much privacy as a sideshow ape at a circus." Learning of his friend's plight, Henry Ford one day sent over a work crew and sufficient materials to build a fence around the perimeter of the sanctuary to help control the crowds. In 1926 public visiting was restricted to the periods April 1-20 and July 1-20. This, of course, did not include Sundays, when the sanctuary was always closed since the Miners strictly observed the Sabbath. (The official observance of the Sabbath continues to this day.) A few years later the restrictions on visiting were relaxed as the public demonstrated a greater respect for the Miners' property and their occasional need for privacy. During the height of its popularity, between 5,000 and 10,000 cars would arrive at the sanctuary on a single day, carrying a total of as many as 15,000 visitors.

Equally impressive as the spectacle of the wild geese were the sanctuary's plants and flowers and the many songbirds that nested there. In fact, flower lovers might have been more impressed by the gardens and flower beds than by the geese themselves. A newspaper reporter wrote in this regard that: "Botanists and professors from a great number of colleges and universities on the continent have visited Jack Miner's home and it has often been said that he has one of the largest out-of-door flower gardens in Canada." At one point, Jack was even labelled the "Luther Burbank of Canada," although he was reported to have demurred with a modest smile that such a comparison "was going it a little too strong."

But so compelling was the aura of the sanctuary that one woman wrote that even the hordes of bees that pollinated the thousands of flowers had fallen under Jack's spell: "There must have been thousands of Bees in this enclosure sipping the honey from the honey-laden blossoms of this paradise, but

Cars crowded the road adjacent to the sanctuary as early as 1915–19 (top), through the 1920s (middle), and into and beyond the 1940s (bottom). (Dr. R.D. Sloane)

Scenes from Jack and Laona's famous flower garden and rose arbour. (Dr. R.D. Sloane)

they neither feared us nor did we fear them, for if the plains are the "Plains of Peace", the entire spot might be called the "Fields of Love"—for love begets love, and even the Bees forget their sting in Jack Miner's paradise of the wild things of the air."

A similar conclusion was reached by the Canadian poet Molly Bevan, who wrote of Jack's "spiritual courage that lay back of the material achievement and prosperity that surrounded him": "His guiding principle seems to be Love—love of the out-of-doors with its teeming life; love of children and their frank trust; love of home and of the homely virtues, and, above all, love of God."

Many people were inspired to write poems praising Jack's sanctuary or his various conservation efforts. Some of these literary works were mailed directly to the Miner home, while others were published in local newspapers and other limited-circulation publications. Most of these efforts were the sort of doggerel that one would expect from amateur authors, but Jack's friendship with the highly regarded Canadian poet Edgar A. Guest did produce some notable odes to Jack's special powers over nature and a touching lament on the occasion of his passing.

A number of visitors travelled great distances to view the sanctuary and meet Jack. These travellers were more often than not ministers who had heard and been deeply moved by Jack's idea to spread the word of God on the wings of wild geese. One such man was the Reverend J. W. Walton, an Anglican missionary on the east coast of Hudson Bay for over thirty years, who travelled several thousand miles to meet Jack and personally deliver bird bands that the native peoples had collected from geese they had killed. A similar pilgrimage was made by a Reverend Campbell in the 1930s. During a one-year furlough this missionary from the Solomon Islands was on his way to England, but had always wanted to see the Ford motorworks and Jack Miner's sanctuary, having learned about the latter through articles in Sunday school papers.

While such long-distance journeys were impressive, possibly the most dramatic visit to the sanctuary took place in April of 1925 when a trainload of wealthy industrialists and prominent conservationists in the party of Pittsburgh magnate Richard B. Mellon arrived. In addition to bank, railroad, insurance, and steel company presidents, the group included a newspaper editor and leading officials of the Pennsylvania Audubon and Humane societies. A local newspaper entitled its story about the visit "A Visit from Croesus: Forty-one Business Men in the Millionaire and Multimillionaire Class Inspect the Miner Sanctuary." It described the travelling arrangements for the group and their activities at the sanctuary in considerable detail:

> The party left Pittsburgh the previous evening in two elegant private coaches with diner attached, running as a special on

the Pittsburgh and Pennsylvania Railroad, arriving in Detroit the next forenoon. They were whisked out to Highland Park and went through the Ford plant for an hour. Their special was ferried over the river and at Walkerville Supt. Black of the P. M. Railway connected up with one of the company's engines and soon had the party on its way to Kingsville, running as a special. Arrived here at 1:30 they were met by the new W.E. and L.B. motor coaches and Bertrand's taxis and taken to Miner's. After the party had been conducted all over the place, saw the geese coming and going to and from the lake, they inspected the Scotch pine, white pine and maple groves, the red cedar windbreak around the ball diamond and other notable features of the sanctuary. They were then taken to the lake to see the wild life. It was unfortunate, however, that only a few white swans remained to be seen, the hundreds that had been disporting themselves for a couple of weeks having gone north to Lake St. Clair. However, there were thousands of geese and ducks and they made noise enough to satisfy anyone that they felt quite at home. After spending some time at the lake, they returned to their coaches and shortly thereafter came up to the King's hotel where Mr. Hall had a nice dinner [for fifty] awaiting.

After the meal the visitors proceeded to toast Jack. One observed that being closer to nature, one was closer to God, and today they had been with "one of God's noblemen." The past president of the Audubon Society of Pennsylvania was particularly impressed by having seen Jack's notions about con-servation being put into action, for he was in effect saving these birds from destruction. The sportsmen in the group were inspired by seeing such large numbers of wildfowl under such favourable conditions at close range. Mr. Thomas Liggett, a wealthy realtor who acted as toastmaster, and Mr. John M. Phillips, Commissioner of Conservation for the State of Penn-sylvania, each gave testimonials that, when taken together, summarized the consensus about Jack's contribution:

What constitutes a successful life? If when one goes out over the bar one leaves the shore more beautiful. Fifty and seventy-five years ago wildlife was super-abundant, but if we are going to leave any of it as a heritage to our posterity, we must follow some such guiding hand as Jack Miner's. Jack is not planting trees for himself, though he may enjoy the work, but he will leave a lasting memorial to posterity when he passes on to the great majority. There are just two kinds of people in this world—just two—they are lifters and leaners. There is only one lifter to every 10 who lean. Jack belongs to the right sort—the lifters . . .

You have taught the world how to preserve the wildlife and in that you have accomplished one of the greatest works the world has ever seen. I am mighty proud of you and you have taught us that instead of being God-fearing, we should be God-loving Christians . . .

After the testimonials the motion pictures of the sanctuary were shown to the great approval of the audience, who applauded at intervals. At the conclusion of the program the group departed and the final portion of the "Visit from Croesus" was again described at some length in the newspaper report:

> At the conclusion, about 11 o'clock, the visitors all went to the P. M. Station to their coaches and retired for the night. The next morning they were up bright and early and took buses for the Sanctuary once more to see the birds coming in from the lake. Later on they returned to their train, leaving here at 10 o'clock. Arriving in Detroit, they started on their homeward trip, only making one stop between Detroit and Pittsburgh, a record run, arriving home in time for tea, no doubt tired but we believe pleased that they had seen for themselves a little corner of Ontario, and shaken hands with their modest friend, Jack Miner.

The reaction of these and countless other men could doubtlessly be summarized by the words of a visitor a few years later in describing the effect of meeting Jack at the sanctuary: "The other day I turned aside from a great city and thirty miles in the country met a man who made a contribution in my life that I doubt I shall ever get over . . . He is a benefactor to the human race."

During the course of his address to this Pittsburgh group Jack had suggested that a sanctuary be established in North Carolina. While it is not clear whether this particular proposal was in fact carried out, there were two projects in the group's home state of Pennsylvania that did ensue from this visit to the Miner sanctuary. Led by Liggett and Mr. James Borland, editor of the Franklin, Pennsylvania, *News and Herald*, a committee from the Pittsburgh group presented a petition to the Pennsylvania Game Commission requesting that a sanctuary similar to Jack's be established in the Pymaturning area, and within a year the Pymaturning Wild Life Refuge was a reality. Similarly, another collection of individuals from the Pittsburgh party took action to save the last stand of white pines in the Keystone State. Inspired by Jack's efforts in Kingsville, they purchased this area known as Cook's Forest for use as a state park.

These particular events are just isolated examples of a similar but much wider influence that Jack had on the increase in the number of wildlife preserves, refuges, and sanctuaries. Jack spoke at meetings early in the history of local chapters of the Izaak Walton League—especially in Iowa, Illinois, Wisconsin, Minnesota, Indiana, and Ohio—to attract attention and members, as well as contribute to the financial solvency of the organizations. One notable contribution in this regard was his assistance to the Wisconsin state chapters in publicizing the drive to transform Horicon Marsh into a state preserve for Canada geese. While Wisconsin chapters of the League ultimately accomplished the task themselves, their efforts were assisted by Jack's support since, as Aldo Leopold, the first U.S. professor of game management and an active Wisconsin

In 1927 Jack feeds Canada geese with the operator of one of the sanctuaries he helped establish in Minnesota.
(Miner Collection)

League member, pointed out: "The Jack Miner Sanctuary is one of the pioneer refuges and has had continual influence in proving the success of the refuge idea."

Jack also used personal contacts to persuade rich and powerful individuals in Michigan and other Midwestern states to build sanctuaries based on his model. One such individual was W. K. Kellogg of Battle Creek, Michigan, of Kellogg's Cornflakes fame. George Hebden Corsan, Sr., had brought Jack's work to Kellogg's attention and Kellogg was so intrigued that he invited him to speak at the auditorium of the Kellogg Sanatorium. Kellogg then visited the Miner Sanctuary personally, and, as Manly describes, that visit was the catalyst for Kellogg's venture into wildlife preservation:

> No man other than Mr. Henry Ford ever came here who became more excited in what he saw than this Mr. W. K. Kellogg. He stayed all night with father and mother in their little humble home and when I arrived the next a.m. father and Mr. Kellogg were up early in the morning watching the early morning flight of the geese.
>
> I can hear him yet saying "Jack Miner, can I have this at Battle Creek?" The result was that Mr. Kellogg had father go to Battle Creek where he took father to a small lake near by and father pronounced it to be an ideal location with the result that within a year upon invitation from Mr. Kellogg he returned to learn that Mr. Kellogg had not only purchased Winter Green, the lake, but some eighteen hundred acres of land—more or less—surrounding the lake, making an ideal acreage for a sanctuary.
>
> The Kellogg Sanctuary soon became famous and father, at Mr. Kellogg's request, would return to Battle Creek at least once a year and he and father would spend the next day at the Sanctuary at Winter Green Lake.

When asked to suggest an appropriate manager, Manly recommended Corsan, who had originally brought Jack to Kellogg's attention. When Mr. Kellogg contemplated retirement to California and asked Jack what he should do about the sanctuary, Manly suggested donating it to Michigan State University, and this was eventually done.

Jack's acquaintance with Kellogg also led indirectly to his association with Drs. Charles and William Mayo of the Mayo Clinic in Rochester, Minnesota. Some patients who had heard Jack speak at the Kellogg Sanatorium went on for further treatment at the Mayo Clinic and spoke so highly of Jack that the Mayo brothers invited him to speak to their patients should he ever be in the Minneapolis/St. Paul area. Manly arranged just such a visit, and a scenario similar to the one with Kellogg quickly unfolded: The Mayo brothers were impressed with Jack's talk, members of their families visited the sanctuary on several occasions, and the Mayos eventually asked for the Miners' assistance in establishing a sanctuary of their own.

Similar results were forthcoming from Henry M. Wallace, a

Overleaf: Jack, seated at the head table (right of centre), was a featured speaker at the Izaak Walton League banquet in Chicago in 1929. (Kaufmann & Fabry)

THE 9TH ANNUAL CONVENTION BANQUET
IZAAK WALTON LEAGUE OF AMERICA
HOTEL SHERMAN, CHICAGO APRIL 24, 1931

noted Michigan lawyer, and Henry B. Joy, of Packard auto-mobile fame. Wallace established the Migratory Bird Refuge of Michigan on his property at Milford, Michigan, and upon his retirement to Florida, with Manly's help, transferred his flock to the Seney National Wildlife Refuge in northern Michigan. Joy established what he called his Joy Ranch in Michigan on the north shore of Lake St. Clair, using seven of Jack's domes-ticated hand-raised, wing-clipped wild goslings. Other U. S. sanctuaries inspired by Jack's work were the Bethel Point Sanctuary in Maine and Lincoln Lake near Ludington, Michi-gan. And according to a 1926 report in *Rod and Gun in Canada*, during a tour through New York and the New Eng-land states, Jack "has continually made a strong plea to the wealthy classes to dedicate their country estates to the birds by making bird sanctuaries of them. More than twenty-five big sanctuaries have been established the last two years by this bird lover's efforts."

Jack also had a hand in the establishment of Quetico Supe-rior Forest International Park in Minnesota and Ontario and the Everglades National Park in Florida. The former was the brainchild of a St. Paul, Minnesota, woman, Frances Andrews, who enlisted Jack's support to convince the Ontario govern-ment of the desirability and practicality of the idea (which he did). Jack was drawn into the latter project through his friend-ship with Mrs. Thomas Edison, who entreated him to inter-vene with President Hoover to support the Audubon Society project, and to help promote the cause in Florida as well.

Jack was just as successful in this realm in Canada as he was in the United States. He assisted both Wallace Havelock Robb and Walter Turner of Belleville, Ontario, in establishing sanc-tuaries, while Reuben Lloyd came to be known as "the Jack Miner of Saskatchewan." But probably the closest attempt to replicate Jack's work was undertaken by John W. Piggott in Bridgetown, Nova Scotia.

Piggott reported looking for Jack's articles in outdoor maga-zines when he was just a boy, and was greatly inspired by his ideas. Jack helped Piggott to establish his Bird Haven Farm in the Annapolis Valley when Piggott was twenty-five years old, and was made Honorary President of Bird Haven Limited in recognition of his contribution. Bird Haven consisted of ten acres of land with a large pond in the centre of it. Piggott had managed to attract snow buntings, goldfinches, and blue-birds, as well as Canada geese to his property, and by 1932 the Montreal *Star* was describing him as "second only to Jack Miner in his work of preserving wild bird life." In that same year he had 6,000 trees of different varieties planted about the grounds with plans to plant 9,000 more. As if the parallel to Jack was not close enough, Piggott also lectured to children in the schools about his work with the birds.

In addition to motivating private citizens to emulate him,

A 1927 letter from an exiled Russian count liv-ing in France who claimed to have established a sanctu-ary in Russia modelled on Jack's. Jack was so well known that an envelope as confus-ingly addressed as this one was able to reach his home.
(Miner Collection)

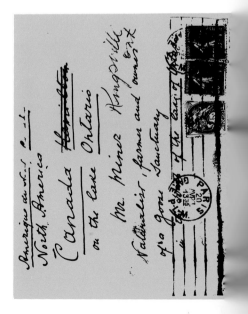

Canada. Hamilton on the lake of Ontario
Mr. Miner. Naturalist and owner of a Goose
Sanctuary in the South of the lake of Ontario.

In the number of the Times (23 Mai 1922) I read a very
interesting article about your Goose Sanctuary in the South of
the lake of Ontario but there was no address so my first letter
came back from Canada without an answer. This time I Wright
to Hamilton but I am not sure its your true address. Perhaps its
Toronto.
I am an enthusiastic Russian lover of birds and the idea of
having a Goose Sanctuary on the lake of the Ilmen in the governe-
ment of Novgorod is my idée fixe. You would make me
happy if you would be so kind as to write me a letter in
which you would point all the necessary details and
methods of organising a Goose Sanctuary. I beg your pardon
for adressing you this letter but I know you will as a naturalist
and lover of birds understand my idea and joy in
receiving from you an answer.   20 April 1926.

                                              France near Paris
        Yours truly,   Varenne St Hilaire
   Count Dmitri Chérémeteff   Avenue du 11 Novembre
                                            N 40 Villa le Roserai

An Honorary Member of the Moscow Association of Lovers of singing
and other wild birds
An Honorary Member of the Russian (Imperial) Poultry Utility Society
Member of the Imperial Russian Geographical Society

     Please answer kindly to the address   France
Cap d'Antibes Villa Donatello

Jack was also successful in having politicians act on his suggestions. He was instrumental in having Point Pelee, a nature area in the vicinity of his home, established as a national park. In the 'teens, Jack with four other members of the South Essex Conservation Club passed a resolution to that effect, and Jack presented the resolution to the Canadian Prime Minister while on a speaking trip to Ottawa. Along with Dr. William T. Hornaday, Jack is considered as well to be one of "the two most influential men responsible for the Migratory Bird Treaty."

Jack was also active in game commissions and wildlife conferences, participating in the national Wildlife Conference in 1919 and serving on the Ontario Special Game Committee in 1931–32 (after declining the committee chairmanship due to the amount of time it would have subtracted from his duties at the sanctuary and on the lecture circuit). But Jack's influence was not limited to North America. In 1927, for example, he received a letter from France written by a count, formerly of Russia, who had read *Jack Miner and the Birds* and claimed to have started a sanctuary in northern Russia based on Jack's principles. And in 1934 Jack received a request from the government of Czechoslovakia for information about his sanctuary system to be used in establishing a number of bird preserves in that country.

Even after his death Jack continued to have an international visibility. The Reverend Bruce Suitor, who as a child had experienced "Uncle Jack's" warmth and later served a period as a minister in Kingsville, reports an incident that verifies this fact. During an assignment in Korea in the 1950s, Suitor had occasion to query a group of schoolchildren about their knowledge of Canada. To his amazement, although they were unable to name the Prime Minister of Canada or identify other prominent Canadians, they were able to go into great detail concerning the exploits and accomplishments of Jack Miner, as well as the activities at his sanctuary.

Jack's bird bands and their use to spread God's word had a largely positive effect. The Western Pennsylvania Humane Society, for example, found them useful in generating public interest in its activities. When the Society held a poster-design contest related to one of its functions in 1934, all award-winning entries and honourable mentions received one of the Miner goose tags that Jack had donated. But as if to prove that any good idea can be put to a bad use, Saskatchewan Premier J. T. M. Anderson cited Jack's utilization of bands for the identification of geese as an example of what he intended by his proposal to use similar identification bands on immigrants to monitor their movements—an idea to which Jack would not have been able to subscribe.

He showed no reluctance, however, when citizens of Essex County formed a conservation organization in 1920 and called it "The Jack Miner League," with Forest H. Conover of

An advertisement for the popular but short-lived Jack Miner League, containing a statement of the League's principles that Jack had set down at the founding members' request.
(Miner Collection)

The JACK MINER LEAGUE STANDS FOR:-

1. What is best for the most people and not for the favored few.

2. The conservation of the Dominion's Forest resources as one of the most important foundations of the country's prosperity and the natural habitat of wild life and the first essential to the continuity of our rivers and water powers.

3. Reforestation of all waste lands and windbreaks and forest borders of at least ten per cent of farming country knowing that the other ninety per cent will become more productive and have the comforts of the windbreaks and timber to their good.

4. Preservation of all remaining marshlands and replanting and maintenance of natural conditions and environments.

5. Preservation and culture of wild flowering and other plant life, as well as other flowering and plant life, that makes our houses into homes more attractive and loveable.

6. At least one Government Sanctuary of at least twenty-five acres in each county and no shooting to be allowed within one mile of it. Lands round the—protective zone to be open to public shooting in the open season. This policy will distribute the wild life more evenly throughout the nation.

7. The Migratory Bird Treaty between Canada and the United States and a small uniform Federally controlled bag limit treating all provinces and states alike.

8. Prohibition of sale or commercialization of game in any way, shape manner or form.

9. Erection of a small observatory on every sanctuary so that the bird lover with his kodak can have first choice without disturbing the birds. Jack Miner knows that the bird lover takes nothing from the shooters, and by encouraging him, his assistance aids the building up of the overflow from the sanctuaries for the shooters' limited toll.

10. Appointment of game law enforcement officers by qualification and not by favor.

11. Practical control of predatory birds and animals.

12. Opposing pollution of streams that is detrimental to food and game fishes and their foods, and for establishment of hatcheries for these species to restock our lakes and streams.

13. More wild nature studies in our schools that our children may become more interested in closer acquaintenance with all forms of wild life, their habits and haunts.

14. Amalgamation of all conservation and wild life protective organizations with a view to uniformity of policy and activities co-operative to one common end.

15. More and better education for all with special attention to God's promise in Genesis 1-26 when he says, "Let man have dominion over all," which Jack Miner has tested out and found to be true. This will eventually bring about more sane and effective legislation in the interests of both national and international affairs and weld us closer together to a mutually beneficial end.

- JOIN -
The JACK MINER LEAGUE

IT IS THE SAFEST INSURANCE AND SECURITY OBTAINABLE FOR YOUR FUTURE, AND YOUR CHILDREN'S FUTURE, RECREATIONAL PERIODS AFIELD.

Leamington as its first President and Edward R. Kerr of Walkerville its first Secretary-Treasurer. While in general the League was an "organization working in the interests of forestry, horticulture, agriculture, economic wildlife, wild-life haunts, and restricted and ethical sports with rod and gun," Jack was asked to write down what he stood for and the constitution was drafted around his principles.

For the first few years chapters of this Canadian version of the Izaak Walton League were confined to Essex and Kent counties in Ontario; but by 1925 there were chapters in Victoria, British Columbia; Winnipeg, Manitoba; Montreal, Quebec; and Hamilton, Ontario; as well as in other parts of British Columbia, Quebec, and Ontario. Also, several existing bird societies had changed their names to that of the Jack Miner League. In 1926 a chapter was established in Belleville, Ontario, and by 1934 the League had spread east across the continent to Prince Edward Island when the "Pioneer Branch of the Jack Miner League of P.E.I." was established. The ultimate goal was the setting up of such organizations throughout Canada with at least one chapter in every province and a representative from each province to be appointed to a national board of directors. In 1930 the League expanded its focus somewhat, forming the "Jack Miner Game Fish and Angling Section" that was designed to protect some fishing areas from commercial nets. But while the League attracted considerable attention in its first years of operation, it lacked an adequate organizational base and eventually disappeared altogether from the conservation scene.

If Jack Miner was given a choice as to whom he could speak and with whom he could interact, he would invariably choose children. Since the days of his Sunday school classes, he had demonstrated a remarkable interest in, and a rare ability to communicate with, young people. As described by his youngest son, Jasper, Jack "definitely showed his greatest delight when he had a small group of children around him and with them holding their attentive little faces up looking into his. . . . he simply received joy from being with them and seeing them and looking at their sweet little faces and listening to their little voices." The feeling seems to have been mutual. "Uncle Jack," as he was known to children of all ages, had the uncanny ability to entrance youngsters when he spoke to them.

Jack, like most adults, believed that children are the hope of the future. He also believed that if he could introduce children to the wonders of nature at an early enough age, they would avoid engaging in the kind of needless slaughter that Jack had perpetrated as a youngster, and would have a good start on the parth to responsible adulthood. But there were perhaps deeper reasons for Jack's intense interest in children, related to the sadder, darker periods of his family history, as Jasper Miner suggests: "It could be that he had such a love for his own little

Opposite: Jack's talks to children inspired many birdhouse-building contests—this one in Peterborough, Ontario, in 1929. (Fred Roy)

Two boys from the School for the Blind in Brantford, Ontario, constructed this martin house after Jack had spoken at their school (ca. 1924). One boy in thanking Jack had said: "Although we have never seen the sun, we are not blind; we can plainly see all you have been telling us." (Miner Collection) girl and boy—little Pearl—and I don't know, we'll say that God works in a strange way. But I think this loss—actually this memory of this sweet little girl that he lost—left him with this [feeling] that he could possibly hang on to her [by paying attention to all these youngsters]."

Whatever the reason, Jack definitely took a special interest in children. He encouraged them to build birdhouses, for he knew that such an endeavour would kindle the love of birds in their hearts. Birdhouse-building contests became a popular pastime for North American youth and Jack Miner was asked to judge many a competition.

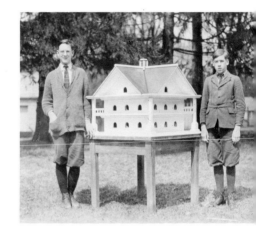

He also reached large numbers of youngsters through his radio broadcasts in the early 1930s. The first half of the thirty-minute broadcast was devoted to children, and numerous radio parties were held in people's homes with as many as fifty children being reported at one gathering. As a result of the broadcasts in 1930, some 35,000 boys and girls were enrolled

Two little girls play with "Beauty", a deer that Jack had trained to come on command (ca. 1925). *(Ford Motion Pictures, Miner Collection)*

The Bailey sisters, neighbourhood children, feed custard to Jack's pet robins in the rose arbour at the sanctuary (ca. 1925). *(Ford Motion Pictures, Miner Collection)*

as members of the Junior Bird Clubs (thereafter called the Jack Miner Junior Bird Clubs), with each child receiving a bird button and educational leaflets on native birds while promising to be kind to birds and to protect them.

While youngsters at his appearances were usually thrilled at the attention he paid to them, Jack would often pay more attention to those who were not there. If he received word that a child had been unable to attend due to illness, he would invariably visit the youngster in his sickbed to cheer him up and leave a goose band inscribed with a biblical verse as a

remembrance of the occasion. John Jasperson was one youngster who received such special attention on an extended basis
when his father, Colonel Fred Jasperson, was a prisoner of war
during World War II: "He wanted to be a helping person.
He wanted to introduce me to the wonders of nature and to
discuss with me the wonders of nature. Always we would be
talking about the outdoors . . . you know it was [always] . . .
Jack, I and nature out there."

In order to make youngsters feel at home at the sanctuary,
he literally turned it into a playground for the children of
Kingsville. With the help of Detroit Tiger baseball star Ty
Cobb, a good friend and a frequent sanctuary visitor, Jack laid
out a baseball diamond on the grounds and encouraged the
formation of a local youth team, "The Barefoot Nine." In the
winter the ponds were cleared for skating and hockey. Jack
trained a young deer to come on command, and young robins
or ducklings could be summoned by tapping a spoon on a
tin dish filled with food. The ducks, geese, and swans that inhabited the ponds were an endless source of interest, and there
were tumbler pigeons that could be enticed with corn to sit
on heads, shoulders, and arms.

A clubhouse that Jack had originally built to keep his own
three boys close to home was still attracting the neighbourhood
children long after his own youngsters had grown up. A visitor in 1939 described the scene as follows:

*A hockey game in progress on
a patch of snow-cleared ice
on one of the Miners' back
ponds (ca. 1925).* (Ford Motion
Pictures, Miner Collection)

Every night, during the summer, with the exception of Sundays,

there's a ball game in progress with Jack Miner himself sitting in the rear enjoying the game more perhaps than those taking part.

The club house is used for banquets and games, and picnics are held here if rain comes to upset other plans. Long trestle tables stretch the full length of the club house, a large fireplace graces one side, and on the walls hang moose and deer heads— trophies of the hunt and numerous animal and bird pictures. In the winter, when the ponds are frozen for skating, boys and girls come here beside the roaring open fire to change their skates.

And John Piggott, who emulated Jack's work at his own sanctuary in Nova Scotia, described Jack's wild goose sanctuary as "just as truly a sanctuary for boys" after witnessing the 1937 annual picnic for underprivileged children that Jack cosponsored with the Lions Club.

Whether on stage in a lecture hall, at home greeting visitors personally, or addressing listeners over the radio, Jack had the conviction and power of personality to impress upon people the importance and necessity of preserving God's creatures. Such charismatic appeal enabled him to make conservation an essential issue in the first half of the twentieth century. However, many wildlife biologists and government scientists found his anecdotal, "unscientific" approach unacceptable, and took exception to many of his ideas, particularly those dealing with the control of predators. Nevertheless, even one such critic was forced to concede that Jack's "greatest contribution was that he reached hundreds of thousands with a simple sincere plea for wildlife conservation."

Opposite: Jack entertains a young visitor on the sidewalk in front of the sanctuary by feeding tumbler pigeons from his mouth (ca. 1936).
(Miner Collection)

All my studies have been in the great out of doors and among the creatures that occupy it; but I am here to tell the world that the more one studies these so-called wild creatures, the closer and closer will they bring him to God Who created them all and blessed them and gave man dominion over them.

6

Let Man Have Dominion Over All

JACK Miner's life spanned a period of human history that was rife with change. Life in North America in the mid-to-late 1800s when Jack was born and growing to adulthood was still basically rural and agrarian. Although individual families such as Jack's might be very large by today's standards, the society as a whole was small-scale and close-knit. People's lifestyles were basically conservative, and traditions were valued highly and adhered to strictly. There was still a sense, albeit largely unconscious, that people must stick together in order to survive against the adversity that could be created by nature and by one's fellow man. But the move toward industrialization and mechanization that took place before the turn of the century, and intensified quickly during the first years of the 1900s, soon altered fundamentally this earlier social scheme. People flocked to the cities that grew by leaps and bounds as urbanization intensified; the mode of social organization moved toward what sociologists have termed "mass society," with the radical changes in relationships and values that such a shift entailed.

Jack Miner witnessed these developments and was touched by almost all of them. He had little trouble adopting the numerous inventions and innovations that were introduced in his lifetime (such as the light bulb, the telephone, indoor plumbing, the radio, and so forth), and he adapted quite well to most of the changes in the social, economic, and political arrangements that took place during this tumultuous period. But Jack held firmly to the attitudes, beliefs, and values with which he had been raised. And nowhere was this more evident than in his approach to nature.

In an age in which society was becoming increasingly secularized and the doctrine of creationism was being successfully challenged by the Darwinian theory of evolution, Jack based his ideas about man's relationship to nature on passages from Genesis and Deuteronomy, and other chapters and verses in both the Old and New Testaments. Consequently, it was almost inevitable that he would come into conflict with the proponents of this new scientism—or "apeism" as Jack liked to

Overleaf: The tame and injured birds required daily attention year round. Jack was happy to oblige (ca. 1938). (Dr. R.D. Sloane)

refer to it. Given these background influences to his thinking, then, it is little wonder that Jack's basic orientation toward the natural world was a combination of an innate respect and love, a desire for harmony among all of nature's components, and a belief in a benevolent control over and wise husbandry of the earth's resources. As a result, Jack's nature and conservation philosophy contained elements of all three of the main North American traditions of environmental thought identified by environmental studies and management professor Joseph Petulla: the biocentric, the ecological, and the economic. This ability to tap some portion of all three traditions may explain partially why Jack enjoyed such widespread popularity with the general public, business leaders, and politicians, while at the same time experiencing disrepute among strict preservationists, university-trained wildlife experts, and government scientists.

The biocentric environmental tradition is based on man's primitive feelings about nature that caused him to fear and respect both the natural world and the unknown power behind it. This orientation to nature has been changed and refined over the years by the forces of civilization and was eventually modified by Christianity, with Jack Miner's approach being one such example. He readily acknowledged the existence of such an omnipotent, unseen power behind the natural order and wondered how anyone else could doubt it. Jack's literal interpretation of God's injunction to man, as contained in Genesis, however, set him apart from others in the biocentric tradition who conceived of all components of the natural world as being on an equal plane. For Jack there was a definite hierarchy, as demonstrated in his statement: "Nature is wonderful; Man is more wonderful; God is most wonderful." Moreover, God gave man "dominion over all," hence "Man is Nature's first assistant, or God's viceroy. What is man without God, and what is God without man? They are—or should be—partners." In Jack's view, then, man occupied a superior position to nature but at the same time was burdened with a special responsibility toward God's other creatures.

In the ecological environmental tradition, more emphasis is placed on the stable functioning of natural systems than on the placement of value in each component of such systems. There is, according to Petulla, a commitment to "a model of scientific understanding of how nature orders itself," and a presumption that nature has a self-regulating mechanism that allows it to re-establish harmony after being subjected to disruption. While Jack's position has the least in common with this particular tradition, and he was notably opposed to the "balance of nature" philosophy, he did demonstrate a certain sensitivity to the desirability of harmony in natural systems. In fact, his sanctuary was based on a complex interaction of its natural components, although Jack had himself introduced many of these components and often "assisted" nature in maintaining a balance.

He silenced his critics by cultivating thousands of evergreens in clay soil where they had never grown before. He planted cedar trees for windbreaks and forest borders, and the berries they produced fed the winter birds. Other trees he planted included different varieties of pines, hard maples, mulberries, and elderberries. He also grew wild grapes and sumach, and cultivated roses and many other kinds of flowers. These sources of food and shelter attracted a multitude of song and insectivorous birds, among them catbirds, song and chipping sparrows, brown thrashers, mourning doves, bluebirds, purple martins, robins, goldfinches, and warblers. Ever resourceful, Jack fashioned birdhouses out of brick and tile from his factory, providing unique homes for bluebirds, purple martins, and wood ducks. And he trapped or shot the animals and birds that would have driven away or destroyed these large gatherings of birds if such predators had been left unchecked.

Birdhouses were located throughout the sanctuary.
(Miner Collection)

Those who work within the economic environmental tradition have been known as utilitarian conservationists, for Petulla notes that they advocate "the 'wisest', most efficient use of natural resources over the longest period of time." Jack Miner was not opposed to men taking the overflow of game as long as it was shot without unfair advantage. He favoured renewing species by restocking and was noted for such efforts with pheasants and bobwhite quail in the early part of the century. He was one of the first people to recognize and speak out against the dangers of pollution and to recommend to various state and provincial governments that they get together to take immediate action before the problem got out of hand. He extolled the scenic beauty and abundant wildlife of Ontario as valuable resources to be nurtured and exploited as a means of bringing needed tourist dollars into the country and the province. And, most importantly, the wildlife of North America was a priceless asset that was to be preserved for the pleasure of the vast majority of present and future populations,

Jack designed these for wood ducks. (Miner Collection)

whose only shooting of wildlife would be done with a Kodak. Although there were traces of all three of these environmental traditions in Jack Miner's conservation philosophy, the dominant characteristic was his unique brand of Christian bio-centrism. As Jack was fond of saying, "I'm not so religious that I won't boil water in a tea kettle on Sunday, but I am a firm believer in the teachings of the scripture and base my reasonings in the field of nature management and control as is outlined in Genesis . . ." Under God's scheme the birds and animals were made before man, but once man was created he was given the power and the responsibility to assist nature.

Jack felt that the balance of nature might apply in theory, but as soon as man had arrived in North America and shot his first bird he had interfered with nature and was required to play a role in balancing it. He believed that God, not instinct, accounted for the innate habits and knowledge that birds and animals possessed, and that even the despised predator was meant to be given free rein in God's great scheme before man upset the balance of things. When two sickly wild ducks, whose lives he had attempted to save, infected his healthy ones with a devastating eye disease, Jack was moved to reflect on the role of predators:

> Now, according to my own experience, if a hawk had come along he would have picked up the weak ones and prevented this disease. So, after all my life's study I am fully convinced that these cannibal birds were put here to destroy the weak and sickly and prevent contagious disease, letting the strong and healthy survive. But man has interfered. He has paid all his attention to the destruction of the food birds and has almost annihilated them and let what we now call their enemies go; or,

in other words, we human beings have combined our forces with the food birds' enemies.

Since Jack viewed the Scriptures as confirmation of his personal experiences and observations, in some respects such directly obtained knowledge was a more important underpinning of his conservation ideas than the word of God as contained in the Bible. The longtime friend who wrote the Preface to *Jack Miner and the Birds* underscored the importance of that direct study in Jack's life: "He was never so happy as when studying the lives and habits of the wild creatures, whether it was the timid field mouse or the lordly moose, the socially inclined chickadee or the elusive Canada goose. Thus did he lay the foundation of the success he has achieved as a hunter and naturalist."

Since Jack had learned so much about nature at first hand, it is not surprising that he encouraged everyone else to rely on a similar approach. He often urged his audiences to not accept his assertions uncritically, but rather to subject them to the test of their own critical faculties. As he noted at one point about the state of the world at the time: "One of the greatest needs today is more men who will do their own personal thinking." And probably due to his great confidence in people reaching the same conclusion as the one to which he subscribed so strongly, he even challenged them to question his beliefs about the existence of God. "Now, readers, I cannot expect anything else than that the foregoing unpolished, blunt statements [about my religious belief and faith] will cause you to stop and think. That is exactly what I want you to do. THINK! And while you are thinking, I want you to be fair with yourself first. Then I know you will be fair to God."

This emphasis on direct experience was one of the root causes of Jack's growing disagreement with and animosity toward scientifically oriented and academically trained wildlife officials. Conservation advocates Lorus and Margery Milne have observed in their Introduction to Robert McHenry's *A Documentary History of Conservation in America* that people in the twentieth century generally have lost touch with nature, and science was among the areas affected in that "even a well-informed person tended to substitute musty research for fresh observation." But although this difference in approach between Jack and those who advanced the ecological perspective was significant, there were other important reasons for this divergence.

One such factor was the growing acceptance of the theory of evolution. After the decision in the Scopes "Monkey Trial" in the United States in 1925, which ruled that the teaching of Darwinism in the schools was not unlawful, the theory of evolution began to make inroads into the educational system. Such a development was viewed as a threat to the traditional religious basis of society, and Jack Miner was among those people who condemned it as such. In explaining his reason for attempting to write about religion—a topic that many people much more learned than he had addressed—Jack observed that he was "persuaded that some of the most highly educated people and deepest thinkers get disgusted . . . when some of our so-called learned try to lead us to believe that we originated from dogs, apes, monkeys, and so on." And, at another point, in reflecting on the impact that being in the great outdoors had on him, he was moved to ask: "How can men who study God's great out of doors, and the multitudes of creatures that occupy it, be intelligent and yet say there is no God? I am told they even write nature books, and ignore this great, loving Power."

In addition to this dislike of the banishment of God from the study of the natural world, Jack was somewhat uncomfortable with his own lack of formal education. The role of the school had changed dramatically since the late 1800s. When Jack was a child, classroom education was not considered an absolute necessity, and children were often allowed or required to stay at home to help with physical labour or seek employment to contribute to the financial support of the household. By the time Jack was a noted lecturer and authority on nature, however, the concept of a minimal level of universal education had become firmly entrenched in North American society. Although the children of farmers would be granted temporary leaves to assist their parents when crucial farm work had to be done, youngsters were normally expected to attend school regularly until they had attained a certain minimum age (which varied across the continent) or had managed to successfully complete an entire elementary school curriculum. The average educational attainment level of the population was consequently much higher during this first quarter of the twentieth century, and many young people proceeded to high school, and even on to college and university, rather than entering the work force immediately upon graduation from public school.

Jack seemed to be highly ambivalent about his own limited "A,B,C education" in this altered milieu. On the one hand, he had enjoyed his lessons in nature's classroom and was proud of the habit of independent thought that such personal experience and observation had engendered in him. On the other hand, he made constant reference to his lack of formal learning, and somehow seemed to regret that the boy who had won the prize as best pupil during the only three months he ever attended school regularly had not had the opportunity or the inclination to further his education. At one point in his writings, as he prepared to present some suggestions for improving the lot of wildlife in North America, Jack paused to beg for his readers' indulgence: ". . . before I go further, I want to apologize for my lack of scholarship, for neglected red hair, freckles and the fragrance of a young skunk catcher, and mother necessity all combined their forces and kicked me out of school. The result is I was educated for ditching, splitting

The schoolhouse in Dover Center, Ohio, that Jack attended for three months in 1878. (Miner Collection)

rails and market hunting." And in another context, he was heartened by a recollection of his mother's earlier advice to him: "I can almost hear her loving voice as, over sixty-five years ago, she looked into my eager, freckled face and, smiling, said, 'Jack, some day you will find that *I* is the first letter in Ignorance.' Yet what can I do? I have no literary education to draw from. Nothing but a few tested facts taken from God's blueprint."

Thus, it is not surprising that he would have disagreements with academically oriented naturalists. His son Manly would write in *The Reader's Digest* about his "most unforgettable character," that "He scorned their 'book learning' and lack of practical experience." And as Jack himself would confess, ". . . I am a very poor reader and have never read a book through in my life"—with the exception of the Good Book, one would suspect. In this impatience with book learning, Jack demonstrated a contempt for one of the basic tenets of modern science and education—namely, that knowledge is important in and of itself, and while a fact or a finding may not appear to have immediate relevance, eventually its importance or utility will display itself. But in Jack's opinion, a fact or information was important only if it could contribute to the improvement of a situation *and* was put into action. He did not believe in "knowledge for knowledge's sake." Statistics for him were just so much useless information: "Don't become only a statistician, because it takes more than a lot of wildlife statistics to save our game. What good is our life going to be towards saving our wild fowl if we are going to spend our entire time in piling up a lot of data and figures that never can be used?" Oftentimes in presenting his action philosophy, he would express his disdain for this academic approach to wildlife: "I am not concerned about the number of specks on the woodpecker's tail, the length of the toenails or tail feathers of an English ring-necked pheasant; I am only concerned about there being more in the fall, for humanity, than there were in the spring."

In many scientific quarters this feeling of contempt was reciprocal. Naturalist Fred Bodsworth would write about Jack as "Billy Sunday of the Birds" in *Maclean's* Magazine several years after Jack's death: "Among the scientists most qualified to judge him Miner was regarded as a naive, but well-meaning crackpot, a dabbler in the scientific field of wildlife management with no understanding of the scientific fundamentals involved." It is true Jack was untrained in all the intricacies of the scientific method, but his curiosity was immense and his powers of observation keen, and he had engaged in research and experiments—albeit crude by the standards of academic scientists—from his earliest childhood days when he pinched the tails off polliwogs to test whether or not they grew to become frogs.

Manly Miner contends that Jack's diary of observations of

the decrease in geese, ducks, and upland game birds between 1882 and 1904, which were a large part of the motivation for the establishment of his sanctuary, would today be called "long range research." In addition, the banding of ducks and geese in large numbers to study their migratory routes was "practical research" that contributed to the passage of the Migratory Bird Treaty. Above and beyond these two activities, which had such far-reaching consequences, Jack conducted a continuous series of smaller-scale research studies and experiments as he observed and interacted with the natural world.

A number of such early experiments were carried out at his home as he attempted to raise bobwhite quail and pheasants to stock the surrounding counties and for export to the United States. He tried different constructions to find the best physical arrangement to encourage the quail to feed. He also attempted to prove that the quail should be protected and propagated since they would help farmers rid their fields of weeds. Covering bags of weed seeds with corn, wheat, and buckwheat, Jack discovered that these birds "scratched right down through the grain and ate the weed seeds first." He also tested out flies, maggots, and a cornmeal custard as foods for pheasants, and eventually devised a pen that allowed him to use Wyandotte hens as substitute mothers for quail, pheasant, duck, and, eventually, Canada goose eggs.

From his observations of predator birds locating eggs in nests when he knew they could not see the eggs, Jack was convinced that birds can smell. And in keeping with his emphasis on people discovering for themselves, he described a small study that a person could undertake to prove this ability of birds to his own satisfaction:

> When it is snowing, take a piece of meat that is cold, and lay it down in the centre of the field. Let it snow under, and if there are crows around see how quickly they will find it! Or if you are in the northern country, throw a piece of meat into the snow and let it drift under; the next morning watch the jay locate it. I refer to snow because it is the best natural cover on earth and will give the fairest test, but if you are where there is no snow to try it out, just take some chaff, straw, or sawdust and cover your bait with that.

After he and his young son Jasper trained baby robins to come when they tapped on a tin dish from which they fed the birds custard, Jack became intrigued with the tameness of robins. Not understanding why the tame ones they banded and which returned the next year would not let him and Jasper near them, he was motivated to study the features of such tameness or lack thereof. In what was almost a classical experiment on the subject, he took two young robins from a nest of four where he knew the parents to be exceedingly tame, and compared their behaviour to that of one from a nest of two that had exceptionally wild parents. The results obtained

Jack sits in one of his rose arbours with his tame robins (1925). (Ford Motion Pictures, Miner Collection)

seemed to indicate some sort of genetic or inherited characteristic: "The birds were all taken the same hour. But the two were tamer in two days than the one was in four."

Jack conducted similar research to determine if the Canada goose would inbreed (he found that they did not), and he used his studies of the vocal communication patterns among families of his pet and wild Canada geese to conclude that birds indeed do have a "language." He also spent many patient hours studying the behaviour of the Canada goose in order to trap and band them. Despite his success with capturing smaller birds, there was a long and challenging period of trial and error before Jack's experiments with different kinds of traps for this wily bird were successful: "The variety of contrivances I made during these seven years! And the blisters there were on my hands during that time, caused from cutting and fitting gaspipe frames and trap-doors and stretching poultry netting over the same, are blisters I will long remember."

An interesting observation would often prompt Jack's "little single-cylinder brain" to start studying a particular nature habit, situation, or problem. But his curiosity was often piqued by a visitor's or writer's question, and especially by what he felt to be mistakes of fact or interpretation. Among many other subjects, such questions and inaccuracies caused him to study in great detail the habits of the moose as well as the behaviour of black and red squirrels in order to settle an argument about whether or not the black squirrel hibernates. But one of the assertions that probably caused him to devise more tests to disprove it than any other was that "wild geese migrate at a speed of 120 miles per hour." In one test he timed the flight of the geese from Lake Erie where they spent the night (and whose departure each morning was marked by gunfire) to his home three miles north. In another, he wired ahead to Hudson Bay when the geese left his home on their northward journey, and had the people there wire back when the geese arrived. And on one occasion he even raced the geese from the lake to his home, measuring their speed against his car's speedometer. In none of these instances did he ever record a flying speed greater than sixty miles an hour, with the average being closer to fifty.

Jack Miner's approach was criticized by scientists nonetheless because it failed to strive for the generalizability of findings, which is one of the principal *raisons d'êtres* of science. As Bodsworth explained the reason for the perceived error of Jack's theories, "he insisted on basing everything on what he saw himself instead of combining his own observations with those of others." But Jack was again unwilling to accept this basic tenet of scientifically oriented conservation because to him wildlife management must of necessity be geared to the specific characteristics of a given situation. Manly argued in this regard on his father's behalf after Jack's death: "It must be stressed how important it is to carry out research in any area where a project is to be conducted," and also "when research is carried out it ought to cover a twelve-month period."

Jack instructs some boys at the Taylor Statten camp (Camp Ahmek) in Algonquin Park, ca. 1927.
(Colin Farmer)

Moreover, Manly would contend, Jack's vast range of experiences over many years of study gave him a broad overview and made him uniquely qualified on many different subjects. He had, after all, spent the first forty years of his life living in the woods. Later in his life, lecture tours took him across the length and breadth of North America for a period of thirty years, and when he was not speaking before the public he would use his time "to study the game of the district, and the conditions of climate, food supply, and other animal life that might affect it." In addition, for fifty years in succession during the fall he camped out on hunting and nature study trips in various areas of Northern Quebec and Northern Ontario, and his summers were often spent helping out at boys' camps, such as Camp Minaki and the Taylor Statten camps in Algonquin Park. Few others, Manly claims, could boast such a depth and scope of experience with nature. "Indeed, it seems doubtful if any man ever spent more hours out of doors in various parts of North America than did Jack Miner. It was the widespread knowledge of conditions and variations in habits of birds and animals derived in this way that enabled him to speak with authority."

Jack learned from this wide range of studies that what might apply in one locale did not in another. One such example was the variation in the diet of the marsh hawk, the study of which Manly Miner describes at some length:

> When my late father was conducting the lecture tours he made for many years, he passed through Wisconsin and Minnesota many times. When at liberty, during the day, he would visit marshes, woods, and farmland. On several of these occasions he found marsh hawks' nests; and examining the refuse about them he saw that the entire diet of the young consisted of crabs, fish, and snakes. He found the same thing at marsh hawks' nests in Manitoulin Island. But here in Southern Ontario, especially in Essex County, inland from the lake and marshes, the marsh hawk is one of the most destructive raptores [sic] we have, preying on such birds as the mourning dove and also on young chickens.

Jack also observed differences in the eagle populations of Alaska and of the rest of North America. The Miners did not have to control these birds with guns at their own sanctuary, and even welcomed the sight of them; yet Manly relates how Jack reported that "in some parts of Alaska, on several occasions, he had closed his eyes and opened them again and saw more eagles in view at one time than he had seen in all his lifetime in Ontario." In those circumstances, local authorities and not someone from faraway should decide the appropriate course of action to follow. But as a cautionary note, Manly would add: "That is not to say that because a few eagles are shot in Alaska, they should be shot anywhere [else] in North America."

One of the topics on which Jack deviated from conservation orthodoxy, as a result of the interplay of his Christian bio-centrism and personal observation, was the demise of the passenger pigeon. If he considered the misconceptions about the moose and other animals to be somewhat off base, he found many of the ideas about the disappearance of the passenger pigeon to be nothing short of ridiculous:

> Right down in my heart, the passing of the passenger pigeon is not as mysterious to me as are the different opinions of writers about its extermination. While I must not condemn the other fellow for his opinions as to what happened to the pigeon, yet I want to say this: If my knowledge of the passenger pigeon, its habits, and the cause of its becoming extinct, are as laughable to other writers as their written opinions have been to me, some of them will surely shake their sides.

Jack rejected the notion that the bird had been wiped out either by habitat destruction or by wanton slaughter, or some combination of the two. He could recall a time himself when flocks 200 feet wide and without apparent end would fly across the sky. By inspecting their nests as a youngster, he determined that a single pigeon produced two eggs four times a year, not the single egg once a year as was commonly accepted.

Given this prolific rate of reproduction and the more limited shooting technology of the time, Jack reasoned, it would have been physically impossible for man alone to have exterminated the bird in such a short period of time. Moreover, they were not normally easy prey and their nesting places were relatively inaccessible—and besides, they were not choice table food for which people would pay much money. These factors, combined with the continued existence of considerable suitable nesting grounds, plus the unusual incidence of dead pigeons that he and his family observed, led Jack to another conclusion: It had been God's will, for ". . . sometimes He not only reduces to a limited number, but He exterminates altogether." From the observation of this phenomenon, and of the periodic death of large numbers of other species, such as snowshoe hare and ruffed grouse, as a result of the pressures created by excess numbers, Jack was led to conclude that man was justified in taking some portion of the stock of wildlife: "This is my reason, conscientiously arrived at, for saying that it is not wrong for man to take a limited amount of wild beavers or wild birds, any more than it is to control our domestic animals and fowl; for if we do not do this, God will."

The extinction of the passenger pigeon, regardless of the reason for it, also played a significant role in Jack's conservation ideas that had him in conflict with other naturalists. This elimination of a major food source for predatory birds, plus man's competition with them for the remaining game species, had, according to Jack, thrown nature out of balance and necessitated corrective action:

> . . . now with ninety-five per cent of their food birds gone,

which includes the Passenger Pigeon, the hawks are left hungry, and the only way to restore nature, or bring nature back to her own, is to reduce them to the same extent that other bird life has been reduced; for remember while a hawk will take a weak, delicate bird first, he can and does catch any he wants to, all except the variety of hawks which include the Red-Tail, Red-Shoulder and Broad-Winged Hawks.

This notion of proportional reduction was broadened by Jack and Manly to include the full range of predators, for "man had upset the balance of nature when he shot wild birds and animals for food when he did not shoot their natural enemies in the same proportion." Crows, blackbirds, hawks, bluejays, and other winged predators had so greatly increased in comparison to the number of "birds we want to live to eat worms, bugs, insects and weed seeds" that the former species had to be reduced. Similarly, man was required to take a role in maintaining a balance between the numbers of deer and the wolves that preyed upon them. Manly describes Jack's notion in this regard:

> If man shot deer for food in Northern Ontario then he felt man should kill the timber wolves that lived on the deer to at least the same proportion. The Ontario Government Officials claim "that 82% of a wolf's diet is red tail deer." Jack Miner would always point out that a female deer only produced one fawn and occasionally two per year, while a wolf reproduced five to six pups, so naturally if nothing was done to control the wolves, they would soon be out of proportion in comparison to the deer population.

Jack's antipathy toward predatory animals was confounded— or perhaps even caused—by his tendency to anthropomorphize animals, creating hierarchies among them and dividing them into good and bad species. He was critical of the way in which writers and advertisers had pictured some of "our most harmless creatures" so that "this accursed 'Little Red Riding Hood' stuff" had made "our children in North America so misinformed that they are even afraid of mice." But he was just as guilty of personifying the birds and animals, although his intent was to create a respect for the admirable ones and a dislike for those he considered reprehensible, instead of a generalized fear of all wild species.

Jack gave names to his pet wild ducks, such as Delilah and Katie, and his favourite Canada geese, such as David and Jonathan and Jack Johnson and his family. He also endowed them with human characteristics and feelings, and, given the closeness that he developed with them and the admiration that he felt, he seemed to relate to them in almost human terms. While Jack looked down on the male mallard duck for being "a lazy drone" and a playboy who "hasn't got a bit more principle than some of us men," he was much impressed by the loyalty, dedication, and fidelity of "our model Canada Goose."

He easily identified with the situations in which the ducks and geese found themselves, especially when they involved family tragedies or triumphs. One such occurrence involved a female duck that had lost its brood to a cat, and had obtained a substitute family from a Wyandotte hen that Jack was using to incubate a nest of duck eggs:

> There she sat in the weeds, about four feet in front of the coop, as still as a corpse, and I was compelled to tremble, for here was the head of a sweet, tiny duckling projecting out of her feathers near her wings. This dear old, broken-hearted mother was sitting here, stealing this hen's ducks as fast as she hatched them, and surely she knew they were not hers, for her ducklings were ten or twelve days old. As I looked at her I thought of the times I had crossed the street to meet some curly-haired child that looked like my sweet little girl did.

He hated to see bears caught by steel traps "because in the spring of the year the baby bears are with out [*sic*] its [*sic*] mother," and he even disliked killing the despicable crow and grackle during the nesting season due to the lingering death to which their young would be subjected. On the other hand, as Jack saw it, the wolf was "the slyest, shyest, shrewdest, strongest-scented and most cunning four-footed animal in North America" that engaged in much "destructiveness and cold-blooded, murderous acts," and deserved to be shot to allow for the increase in numbers of the more docile and vulnerable red-tail deer. And skunks were "regular Brighams . . . which display[ed] more of the survival-of-the-fittest, dominating, cruel ways" than any other creature Jack knew. But as if to demonstrate that the directive of Job to learn from the beasts and the fowls was another of God's promises that had been fulfilled, Jack described a situation in which predators (two bald eagles) had menaced some feisty Canada geese at his sanctuary, but nothing untoward ultimately occurred:

> Yes, they apparently settled by arbitration. When I saw how it turned out my heart bubbled over with more love than ever for these two beautiful birds, and as I started for the house I couldn't help but thank Almighty God for the Canada goose and the American eagle, and ask Him to hasten the day when this whole world mass of humanity will settle their differences as these lovely birds did on this occasion.

Normally, however, such predator-prey confrontations were not settled so amicably, and invariably the predator emerged as the victor. In this usual scheme of things, Jack would generally side with the prey against the predator. Hawks, owls, starlings, crows, grackles, English sparrows, weasels, skunks, raccoons, foxes, and wolves were some of the birds and animals he sought to control, despite the fact that he had kept many of them as pets when he was a youngster. He used conventional pole and jump traps, and built specially designed ones of different sizes to capture the birds of prey that haunted the sanctuary. He also devised elaborate schemes to signal their presence. John Jasperson, who as a child spent many hours with Jack at the sanctuary, describes one such arrangement:

> He had a system where he had grackles and robins and blue-jays all working together as a team. There'd be a tree set up with decoys on the top, then a couple of cages to the side with maybe a pair of pigeons or doves, and grackles and robins off to the other side. Nearby he'd have the bluejays that were the alarm clock.
>
> The hawks would soar over, see the doves, try to get at them in the cage, then go over and sit on a post. The bluejays would set up a raucous alarm and out would come Jack and finish off the marauders to protect his birds.

Jack also used a more passive approach to the same problem. He gathered hawthorne trees and planted them in large open fields. When fully grown, they provided protection and housing for songbirds. The trees grew so thick that hawks, owls, and other predators were unable to get in and kill their smaller prey.

Crows and grackles were a problem at the sanctuary due to their vast increase in numbers and their limitless penchant for the eggs of robins and ducks. Jack perfected a trap to capture these predators in large quantities, and proposed to turn these

This blizzard-like effect is the result of thousands of star-lings flying around the sanc-tuary (ca. 1931). (Ford Motion Pictures, Miner Collection)

Jack's legendary crow trap was built along the lines of his goose trap but was even more successful, catching 500 at a try (ca. 1928).
(Dr. R.D. Sloane)

"black murderers" over to trap-shooters "so what is now the crow nuisance will be turned into a sport." The crows were to be given a sporting chance by being released from five unknown traps at twenty-five to thirty yards rise. A shooter would be fined for birds he missed. Such fines would then "be used for buying up old, faithful horses which will be humanely destroyed and used for bait to decoy more of these old, black Pharaohs to their just doom." Jack's trap was such a success that Manly reported as many as 200 letters in one day requesting the plans for it, and a total of 10,000 such requests from all over North America and foreign countries. To meet such demands, they turned the design over to the United States government, which had the Biologic Survey draw up plans and prepare condensed specifications.

Starlings also caused incalculable damage at the Miner sanctuary. Not native to North America, this bird was introduced from Europe in the late 1800s and soon spread across the continent. It was not until 1925 that Jack welcomed the first three to the sanctuary, but within five years starlings had eaten all the food for the bobwhite quail, driven out the vast majority of purple martins, mourning doves, and redheaded wood-

peckers, and their droppings had killed over 2,000 twenty-foot-high white and Scotch pines that had been growing on the grounds for fifteen years and their droppings were germinating huge weeds in the place of those beautiful evergreens. Jack declared war on these pests and built what he called a "Scotch Success Starling net or trap" (due to its great capability at little expense). In the summer of 1931 he caught and destroyed over 17,000. That was only the beginning, however: "But bless your life, there were a million that came to their funeral! Then the Italians of Windsor came down with a net and under our supervision they caught, smothered, and trucked to Windsor approximately 200,000. They were used to feed the hungry." Some 1,500 shotgun shells had been fired off to try to drive the starlings away before this drastic action was taken, but that effort was to no avail. Despite such massive killing, another 25,000 were caught and despatched in June and July of 1932.

Such practices against predators at his sanctuary, and his pronouncements against them in the press and from the public platform provoked the ire of those naturalists and wildlife experts who believed in allowing nature to balance itself. They condemned Jack at every opportunity for what they perceived to be the wanton destruction of these equally valuable birds and animals, and accused him of interfering with the mechanisms that existed in the natural world for re-establishing equilibrium. To Jack, leaving everything to nature was a "do nothing, have nothing policy," as well as a rejection of God's dictum of man's "dominion over all."

During the course of this continuing controversy, Jack attempted to remain as calm and detached as possible. He would mention, for example, that "Several of my most particular friends who do not see eye to eye with me on the hawk question . . . are among my best friends just the same . . ." Moreover, he frequently made a more general plea for the healthy acceptance of honest differences of opinion: "If we don't all see alike on this matter, please don't let our different views make us enemies because I know some of the best lifts I have got in this world has [*sic*] been friendly, constructive criticism and explanation." But Jack felt strongly about his beliefs and values with regard to these matters and he had, by his own admission, a "crimson disposition." Therefore, it was to be expected that Jack occasionally would make intemperate remarks or suggestions. The English sparrows that had driven the barn swallows out of his brick and tile factory and that he blamed for the decrease in the bluebird was, for example, labelled a "flying rat" and a "little, domineering Bolshevik." On one occasion as a friend dissected a shrike, Jack advised all present: "He is a bad one; always shoot him on sight." And in his report to the Ontario Special Game Commission in 1932, he recommended that "crows should be killed at every opportunity in any way or method possible to control them."

While arguing for increasing the cost of hunting licences to raise the wolf bounty in Ontario, Jack similarly advocated that people "[e]xterminate the wolf," and mentioned "the great satisfaction" he had experienced in killing a timber wolf. On other occasions he said he "could have burned that owl [that killed his pet goose Jonathan] at the stake with a good heart," and stated that if the bald eagles that were menacing his geese had touched any of them he " . . . would have knocked a hole in one big enough for a dog to jump through." In addition, in discussing the Cooper's and Sharp-shinned hawks that, in the spring on their return from the South, attacked the cardinals and chickadees at the sanctuary, Jack would say: "I didn't feed these cardinals all winter to feed a bunch of bird murderers. We kill murderers of [the] human family, why not shoot the murderers of the valuable weed and insect eating bird family?"

Such remarks simply served to inflame his critics. They charged him with being provocative and irresponsible. Jack was accused of spreading propaganda since he was condemning a whole family of predator birds because they happened to be destructive in one location. A former adherent to Jack's philosophy, who was to establish a refuge for hawks and owls, characterized Jack's use of the Bible as justification for his campaign against predators as "nothing short of blasphemy" and, reversing an earlier trend, wrote a poem *rebuking* Jack's attitude toward the hawk and owl. Others claimed that predators had been put on earth for the useful purpose of acting as a controller of the weak and the sick to ensure the strength of succeeding generations, and that from the economic point of view

Six-year-old Jasper Miner inspects a tile bluebird nest (1917). (Dr. R.D. Sloane)

birds of prey on the whole do more good than harm. Jack's campaign from that viewpoint was "fanatical and economically harmful."

Others referred to his views as "narrow and bigoted." Jack was accused of not affording the birds at his sanctuary adequate protection and simply being in the unfortunate predicament of being located on the hawks' migratory route. His views were described as misinformed and based on faulty research that neglected the work of experts. Former supporters, such as the Audubon Society, charged Jack with making "bald statement[s], for which he had absolutely not the slightest substantiation of evidence," characterized his attempt to preserve certain birds as "a sentimental act," and labelled him "a lopsided conservationist." A Toronto naturalist found Jack's pronouncements to be "a highly prejudiced indictment of hawks and owls" and noted that they were not Jack's "exclusive property to be trapped and slaughtered at pleasure."

Someone else contended that if, in isolated instances, some predators had to be killed, it should be done quietly and not "shouted from the house tops." This sentiment was expressed at greater length in a letter to the Toronto *Telegram* in 1930. Basing his views on a publication entitled *Framing the Birds of Prey* by New York naturalist David Quinn, the letter writer decried the impact that Jack's views would have on others:

> It is unfortunate that an army of gunners throughout Canada and the United States, knowing Miner's antipathy and pet aversion to predators, eagerly accepts as gospel truth the misleading statements he makes regarding these birds and respond by engaging in a campaign of slaughter on their own initiative.
>
> I am convinced that Jack Miner's well-intentioned program of conservation is defeating its own end, and until he changes his tactics the destruction of our most valuable birds of prey will go on at a pace much to his satisfaction.
>
> The untold harm that Jack Miner's anti-hawk and owl propaganda has already accomplished will take many years of patient, educational effort on the part of the unprejudiced to undo and teach the younger generation that hawks, owls and eagles, as a family, are every bit as interesting and deserve the right to their undeniable place in nature as any 100 percent beneficial song bird that ever dined in Jack Miner's exclusive sanctuary.

Many of Jack's supporters on this issue were farmers who wanted to protect their crops and livestock, and hunters and sportsmen who wanted to ensure adequate stocks of game birds and animals. Given their strong vested interest in this matter and their lack of broad knowledge in comparison to Jack's about the role of predators in specific locations, this particular critic's concern had a great deal of validity.

At most times Jack seemed quite concerned about the impression that his views would have on others. He took pains to indicate that in assisting nature he sought to control various predators, *not* exterminate or eliminate them entirely. The writer of the Preface of *Jack Miner and the Birds*, from his experience learning to hunt with Jack, noted that he exhibited an enlightened sense of responsibility toward the entire nature world:

> What impressed me most, perhaps, in the days of my novitiate was the determination with which he pursued a wounded bird. He would spend an hour ferreting out a cripple rather than leave it to die in misery, or become the prey of its natural enemies, owls, hawks or vermin. He invariably re-piled the logs and brush he had dislodged in his efforts to retrieve a wounded bird. And this is but one evidence that a keen sense of justice, a full regard for the rights of all living creatures, are conspicuous traits in Jack Miner's character.

Jack appeared to realize the danger that uncritical adoption of his views on predators by shooters would create, especially with regard to hawks. He warned at one point: "First of all let me say that the larger the hawk, the more anxious the majority are to shoot him. This is a mistake. It is the medium-sized hawk that is the worst." In another context, as an antidote to this overreaction, Jack noted: "While I would not like to see the cannibal birds become extinct, yet I would be pleased to see them decreased the same as our other birds have become during the last forty years." And as if to demonstrate the truth of this attitude toward predators in general, he reported that he regulated the trapping of weasels that killed his pheasants according to their population: ". . . for three seasons in succession I got over fifty weasels each year. But now they are so nearly exterminated that we only keep one [rather than three] weasel platform[s], as we call them, and catch two or three weasels a year."

His most passionate expression of this approach of limited rather than total reduction of predator numbers came in his discussion of hawks.

> Dear people, don't think I am one who wants to kill or exterminate any variety of bird. The real itching of my trigger finger has been gone for over half my life. As proof of this, my home surroundings is one continuous song of our insectivorous and choicest and most loveable birds that can be selected, brought about through controlling their enemies. Yes, I belong to the humane society and if a boy were to start killing and torturing birds, as their natural enemies do, our humane society will at once check him up. Do we think more of the hawks and owls than we do of our own rising generations?

In the years since Jack's death, Manly Miner has been forced to reiterate this point of view on numerous occasions in order to counteract the continuing misrepresentations and misunderstandings of Jack's position, as exemplified by the following statement from a 1969 article: "Scientists, with exceptional unanimity, are agreed also that Jack Miner was mistaken in one of his cherished views, namely, that *all creatures of prey should be pursued relentlessly and killed*" (emphasis added).

The topic that created the most conflict between Jack and the balance-of-nature proponents was this very issue of the control of hawks. To answer their critics, Manly and Jack devised an empirical study to demonstrate that hawks were more destructive than beneficial and therefore should be reduced proportionately to the decrease in game and other nonpredatory bird numbers. Manly describes the background to and conduct of the study:

> . . . between 1920 and 1930 father had expressed himself so strongly along the lines stated above [regarding the proportionate reduction of predators] . . . that a certain group of bird watchers (you know the type I am referring to) kept the letter boxes of the daily newspapers full doubting father's statements of how the above species of hawks and owls were keeping our weed seed eating and insectivorous birds from increasing. These letter writers all said these hawks lived on mice when I from a boy had seen father open the crops and stomachs of various hawks that were filled with feathers of warblers and other small birds so I conceived the idea myself to send the hawks he shot to the Royal Ontario Museum in Toronto to examine their stomachs. I contacted the officials of The Royal Ontario Museum and they were very cooperative and always have been. I conceived the idea of packing the specimens in common salt to preserve them until they reached the Museum two hundred and fifty miles away.
>
> Father then went a mile away from our Sanctuary so this certain type of bird watchers . . . couldn't say the Sanctuary attracted the birds and when these hawks were migrating, for research purposes he shot these hawks, brought them home and I packed them, prepaid the express and sent them to the Toronto laboratory of the Museum . . .

Jack holds a hawk that came too close to his birds (ca. 1934). (Dr. R.D. Sloane)

The results of the museum's analysis confirmed the Miners' contention, but their critics were neither convinced nor silenced. Some pointed out that the study was restricted to the summer months instead of covering a full twelve-month period, since animals' diets vary over the course of a year as climatic conditions change (which is a point Manly himself has advocated). Others noted that the sample was not representative of all hawks because it contained large numbers of two varieties that are conceded to be the most destructive to small birds. It was also pointed out that these partial results contradicted the findings of a more comprehensive study previously conducted. But Manly was ready for such criticisms. He replied that the study of hawks during the summer was designed to counteract earlier studies, which had neglected that period since researchers had not thought of using salt to preserve specimens, and therefore had not bothered to study stomach contents during the hot weather, when conditions provided a diet of small birds and animals. As for the lack of representativeness of the full range of hawks, Manly pointed out that this was the reality of the situation at the sanctuary and that the larger

These hawks were sent by Manly Miner to the Royal Ontario Museum in 1931 in order to obtain an independent analysis of their diet.
(Dr. R.D. Sloane)

hawks were not shot since they were known to be harmless to the prey with which the Miners were concerned, and only predators caught in the act of destruction were taken. Manly also observed that the more comprehensive study to which others referred as authoritative had been conducted many years ago in Washington, D.C., and was therefore not applicable to the conditions within which the Miners operated. (Several years after Jack's death, Manly indignantly responded to suggestions that Jack had killed some small birds himself and stuck them down the hawks' throats by saying if anyone had tampered with the hawks' stomachs it must have been the biologists who did not believe what they were finding.)

The adverse reaction continued nonetheless, and among the critical publications generated in response was a pamphlet by the Brodie Club of Toronto. When Jack returned from one of his speaking trips to New York City, he informed Manly that through his host, M. Hartley Dodge who was a trustee of Columbia University, he had met and been invited to a Columbia University roundtable at the home of Dr. Nicholas Murray Butler, the president of that institution. Manly was inspired to send both Jack's article and the Brodie Club pamphlet to these gentlemen for an unbiassed assessment. In a few weeks' time the two articles were returned, with the Brodie Club pamphlet having the name of Jack Miner underlined in red wherever it appeared. The only comment that Dr. Butler and the Columbia professors made was: "The subject of the Brodie pamphlet seems to be Jack Miner and not the hawks."

In light of such *ad hominem* arguments, Jack's general disdain for the academic approach to nature, and his short fuse when it came to disagreements, it was inevitable that he would respond in kind. Consequently, Jack's speeches and writings were riddled with references to and examples of the foolishness of such an approach to conservation and wildlife management. Jack often remarked, for example, that a person should "get all the education you can and then add the learning." He also frequently offered the opinion that: "You learn ornithology, biology, zoology by reading, but you learn wildlife management by doing." Or in the same vein: ". . . a man might go on to an agricultural college all his life but reading a textbook won't take the weeds out of one's garden or farm crop." More generally Jack would say, "Let us apply more commonsense and less nonsense."

Between them, Jack and Manly could produce a litany of incidents of the ignorance of so-called educated and learned people: the editor of a state conservation magazine who misidentified a photo of an eagle as a marsh hawk, recalling Jack's remark that "some wildlife biologists don't know a chipmunk from a chickadee"; a wildlife Ph.D. who visited the Miner sanctuary with his class and informed Jack that, according to a textbook, blue and snow geese do not crossbreed despite the evidence of the by-products of such crossbreeding before his very eyes; another such expert who pronounced some sickly ducklings to have a complicated textbook disease when all they had was lice from the Plymouth Rock hen that had hatched their eggs; the wildlife biologists (whom the northern guide and trappers called "bugologists") who did not know that the bull moose shed its horns every winter; and the wildlife biologist who, after he consulted Jack about how to save the swans from going over Niagara Falls and was told to fire guns off to scare the swans before they went over the falls, was found to be having the guns fired *after* the swans had been swept over them. This final example prompted the following exchange between Jack and Manly: "I said to my father, 'This professor has his Ph.D.' Father said, 'What does that mean?' and I said, 'Doctor of Philosophy.' Father said, 'I thought it meant Phenomenally Dumb.' So every time I have a Doctor of Philosophy honor us with a visit I think of my father's interpretation of Ph.D."

Given such experiences with these educated people, then, it is not too surprising that Jack would brag that when he had studied the wild creatures as a young boy, he "knew them and their habits but not their college-given names, and I am persuaded that today there are many with university degrees who know their names but not their habits." And when he was being criticized by such formally trained individuals, he could gain solace and encouragement by recalling his mother's advice: "Great how some men can give advice on running a bird sanctuary to raise birds and control them, and possibly they had the blind down nearly the whole year to keep the sun from dazzling their eyes. Mother always said, 'an old maid could give you more free advice on how to raise a family then [*sic*] ten successful mothers.' ”

This antagonism between Jack and university and college naturalists was not completely representative of the relationship between Jack and the general educational community not connected professionally with the study and administration of conservation matters. He was frequently invited to speak and lecture to university and college gatherings, both in informal settings such as the Columbia University roundtable, and at more formal, large-scale gatherings such as the extended tour he made to several Illinois universities in January, 1930. He also addressed gatherings of elementary and high school teachers, such as the Ontario Educational Association Convention

For the vast majority of people, this was the accepted image of Jack Miner.
(Miner Collection)

at Convocation Hall in Toronto in April, 1920. And in 1926 Jack had the honour of having a quotation of his incorporated into a final examination paper for a course at the University of Toronto. Professor W. S. Milner of the Department of Greek and Roman History had been so impressed by the description of Jack's philosophy as it was reported in the Toronto *Globe* that he set the following question for his fourth-year classics class on "Aristotle's Politics and History of Philosophy": " 'If you are privileged to live in the country you can make your home into a little earthly heaven by interfering with the balance of nature, as you call it, but as I deem it, assisting nature.' What would Aristotle have to say? Mr. Miner relies upon Genesis 1:21–26 and 28 for his doctrine. Upon what does Aristotle rely?"

The newspaper account then stated Professor Milner's rationale for making the comparison: "Aristotle and Jack Miner have the same basic ideas in their writings, according to Prof. Milner. Merely transpose the words 'imitate' and 'assist' in the writings of Aristotle and those of Jack Miner and the meaning is unaltered."

Moreover, if Jack was at all worried about his lack of formal education he need not have been—at least according to the teachers themselves. An article about him in the *Canadian School Board Journal* in 1932 described him as a striking example of a self-educated man. It pointed out that a person can be educated without having a formal education, but cannot really be fully educated unless he undertakes to learn by himself. There is too much emphasis on the part that colleges and universities play in the process, the article continued, and the enlightened person recognizes that learning never ends "until the curtain drops." The conclusion is a testimony to the educational value of personal observation and experience and of doing one's own personal thinking:

> He must be classed among the pioneers and prophets who find out things, become the teachers of others, and the writers of books. Jack Miner is not a follower but a leader. He is always breaking new trails and surprising the public with new ventures. Perhaps formal education in school and college would have left him "cribbed, cabined and confined". Here is a man of strength, initiative and originality.

These qualities were readily recognized by the general public, politicians, and by many, although not all, wildlife and conservation experts and authorities. As Manly Miner observed, the "common people [are] in many cases more interested in sound Conservation" such as Jack preached and practiced than the grand theories of academic naturalists. By framing his ideas and suggestions in terms that the public could relate and respond to, Jack was able to have a much greater impact than the formally trained experts. Alan B. Baker, Outdoor Editor of the Sudbury *Star*, put it this way in a 1955 column about Jack:

> You may go to school all your life, acquire as many degrees as a thermometer and possess a library of textbooks and works of reference and yet fail of achieving your purpose if you have not practical experience; if you have not, by actual performance, so enriched and disciplined your mind as to be capable of producing the practicable system.

Jack had accomplished this task and his efforts were widely acknowledged. Irvin S. Cobb, one-time outdoor writer for *The Saturday Evening Post*, called him "the greatest practical naturalist on the planet." United States Senator Harry B. Hawes described him as "one of the very best minds devoted to sane conservation . . . [who] not only had a vision, but . . . was practical. He did things." Moreover, as Colonel H. J. Heasley, President of the National Canadian Conservation Club, noted: "Jack Miner was a very farsighted man . . . He was frequently at variance with the teaching of some of our natural history professors, but so frequently turned out to be right that he became [*sic*] to be looked upon as an authority." This sentiment was echoed in a letter to the editor in the Windsor *Daily Star* in response to an editorial about the fiftieth anniversary of the Miner sanctuary: ". . . the late well-beloved Jack Miner was—and still is—far ahead of the times, and of the so-called wildlife scientists who have tried to upset his contentions and observations—and failed in all respects."

At the time of his death in 1944, newspapers across Canada carried tributes to Jack, noting the practical contributions he had made. The Toronto *Daily Star* wrote that Jack "probably did more to protect wildlife in Canada than all the schoolroom advice which was given in the same period" and also made "a substantial contribution to scientific knowledge." The Exeter *Times-Advocate* noted: "He was a genuine naturalist, rather than a man of theories. What he spoke of he knew at first-hand . . . He was an out-and-out independent thinker." To the Montreal *Gazette* he represented "the accumulation of an unrivalled fund of first-hand knowledge on [the] nature, capacities and habits [of wild birds]." And for the New Glasgow *News*, "He was a practical teacher and, to him more than any other, goes the credit for educating the people of this continent to the value of conserving wild life."

The Honorable Seth Gordon of the Pennsylvania Game Commission put it this way: "Jack Miner left behind a monument of accomplishments in his chosen field that will always stand as a beacon light for the rest of us to shoot at. I know of no person in all of North America who did more to promote the Conservation of our migratory waterfowl and to encourage the establishment of refuges for these birds than Jack Miner." And Dr. Harrison F. Lewis, former Chief of the Canadian

Wildlife Service, expressed similar sentiments in 1949:

> The most famous name in the annals of Canadian Wild Life Conservation is that of the late Jack Miner. Jack Miner enjoyed wild creatures, he thought and acted to meet their needs and he made outstanding use of his exceptional gifts to enlist several millions of people as supporters of Wild Life Conservation. Much of the present day recognition of the value of wild life preservation stems from the work of Jack Miner.

Perhaps the greatest tribute of all came from the Right Honourable Mackenzie King, Prime Minister of Canada, who had been much taken with Jack's approach to conservation. After acknowledging Jack's contribution to wildlife research through his pioneer banding work, Prime Minister King noted: "The great work done by the late Jack Miner, our beloved naturalist, is an example of a happy combination of theory and practice with commonsense applied which has made Conservation practical. Jack Miner not only preached Conservation but he made a practical demonstration." These sentiments recalled the words King had used to introduce Jack at a speaking engagement in Ottawa fifteen years earlier: "Jack Miner enjoys

Prime Minister Mackenzie King was a long-time supporter of Jack Miner and he echoed the sentiments of most politicians. (Miner Collection)

CNT 6126

R X 49 DL DL

OTTAWA, ONT. 950AM APRIL 10TH 1938

JACK MINER ESQ,

KINGSVILLE, ONT.

PLEASE ACCEPT MY HEARTIEST CONGRATULATIONS UPON THE CELEBRATION TODAY OF YOUR SEVENTY THIRD BIRTHDAY ANNIVERSARY I TRUST THAT YOU MAY BE VOUCHSAFED MANY MORE YEARS OF HEALTH AND STRENGTH IN WHICH TO CONTINUE THE SPLENDID WORK WHICH YOU HAVE CARRIED ON FOR MORE THAN A QUARTER OF A CENTURY.

W.L. MACKENZIE KING.

1005AM

the goodwill of everybody, his Sanctuary and Conservation efforts are not only enjoyed by the birds but by humanity. If Jack Miner's conservation program has any critics what do the critics have to show?"

Jack holds two newly hatched quail: "Let man have dominion over all." (Ford Motion Pictures, Miner Collection)

Conditions in the world have changed greatly since Jack died, even more so than when he was at the height of his career and spreading his conservation ideas across the continent in the 1920s and 1930s. The pollution that Jack was so concerned about as a potential threat to wildlife has turned out to be a real menace to various bird and animal species. Habitat destruction has continued as a source of pressure on our wildlife resources despite some successes in saving wilderness areas and wetlands. One hopeful sign, from Jack's perspective, would be that wildlife management has accepted the notion of the need for man's intervention to maintain the balance of nature, and has increased the emphasis on practicality while at the same time making more use of research and data.

In this regard, the Canadian Wildlife Federation has defined wildlife management as "the art of manipulating wild animals or their environment for the purpose of achieving some predetermined objective" and conservation as "the achievement of desirable management objectives, or the culmination of long term efforts to maintain wildlife populations at sustainable levels, through wise use and proper husbandry." And in their approach to wildlife management, modern naturalist officials have rejected the ecological "balance of nature" approach in favour of a combination of utilitarian/economic and biocentric approaches (but without the obvious Christian element of Jack's philosophy):

> The preservationists' concept of a balanced environment ignores the reality of man/wildlife conflicts, the dynamics of wildlife populations, and the extent to which man has and will continue to intervene in the natural process. Wildlife cannot be stockpiled like goods on a shelf. It is a vital biotic force which responds to stimulation. Conscientious management, and a strong commitment to conservation are the only ways we can ensure that wildlife will always have a place in the world, and share the environment with us.

Despite such changes in orientation, degradation of the environment caused by pesticides and mercury have threatened with extinction such predatory birds as the peregrine falcon, the bald eagle, and the osprey—birds that at any earlier time Jack might have advocated controlling but in the current environment would be doubtlessly fighting to save. As far as the over-all current attitude toward predators is concerned, Jack would probably have no difficulty accepting it as described by naturalist J. J. McCoy: ". . . the general trend and thinking is toward a middle-of-the-road attitude in predator control; that is, predators can be controlled without exterminating them and with minimal damage to other wildlife."

Jack would also be an ardent opponent of acid rain that has killed many lakes and threatens many more in the midst of our breathtaking northern woods. For Jack, such natural features were not only a source of aesthetic and spiritual pleasure but also an economic resource that could attract valuable tourist dollars into the country. And in the greatest of all ironies, he would be confronted with the widespread increase of the Canada goose to the point that they are a nuisance in many parks and golf courses across North America. But Jack would take all of this in stride, and would relish the challenge that such current conditions presented. For he derived his greatest satisfaction from doing his own personal thinking, based on his direct observation and experience, to determine the best ways to maintain the balance of nature as God prescribed when He gave us "dominion over all."

. . . work consists of what you are compelled to, and don't want to, do. And although I have moved hundreds of thousands of tons of clay with my own backbone and hands, yet I have never done any work. . . . Yes, I am living because I want to . . . and am going to continue to live for another hundred years, or die in the attempt!

7

A Legacy to the World

J ACK Miner's boundless and infectious enthusiasm for nature, and the conservation of it, lasted to the very end of his days. Although his public lecture career ended in the late 1930s, due to the unbearable physical demands it placed on a man in his mid-seventies, Jack continued to work around the grounds of the sanctuary, feeding and caring for the geese, tending his gardens, writing about his views on nature, life, and God, and hosting the crowds of visitors who still flocked to his home. It is fitting that on November 3, 1944, he died doing what he loved best and for which he was so revered by the world: ministering to the needs of the thousands of Canada geese that had stopped at his home on their southward migration.

Despite the worldwide recognition and acclaim and numerous awards and honours that Jack had received throughout his life, he never took credit himself, always thanking God for the successes He had bestowed on him. Jack remained forever a simple human being for whom the homely virtues were paramount. He made constant reference with pride to his humble origins and always contended, "The smaller the house, the bigger the home." Moreover, although he had met and been befriended by many of the privileged and the powerful of the times, he was not impressed by social position and treated the lowest individual on the social ladder with the same kindness and respect as he did the highest—and expected the same genuine treatment in return.

Jack was most comfortable when he could wear his old tattered working clothes while carrying out his duties around the sanctuary grounds. However, Manly made sure that his father was properly groomed when on tour or formally entertaining around the sanctuary. He arranged for a New York City tailor to make what became an almost trademark mackinaw sport suit for Jack (in two colours of green plaid), and had Jack's leather boots made in St. Paul, Minnesota. When Jack received his first major request to lecture outside the local

Overleaf: Wild Goose Jack liberates a Canada goose after it has been banded (ca. 1929).
(Dr. R.D. Sloane)

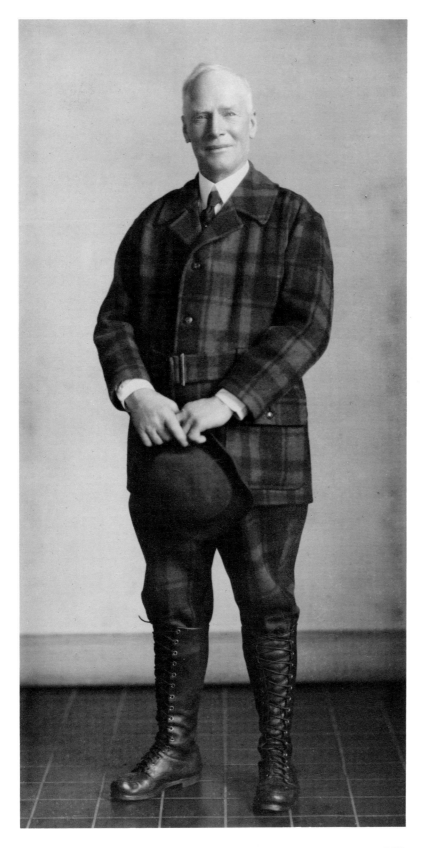

A portrait of Jack (ca. 1928) wearing his trademark mackinaw suit and high leather boots, clothing that Manly had custom-made in the United States. (Miner Collection)

Essex County area, Manly arranged for a proper suit for Jack to wear:

> I said, "Father, a black suit with a white shirt and a black tie is always appropriate at any occasion," and we went downtown and ordered a black suit made out of the same cloth as a black tuxedo and from there on to 1940—some thirty years during his lecture career—he would get a new black suit twice a year and it was in such black suits he appeared when he addressed the outstanding gatherings.

Although Jack may have felt properly dressed in such an outfit, it seems clear he did not feel fully at ease in it. He was fond of observing that his family was so poor all the children were born barefoot, and Jack continued to do without footwear until he and Ted began to frequent local social gatherings during their late adolescent years. But Jack's feet had been broadened by years of running barefoot in the woods, and did not take kindly to the confinement of store-bought shoes:

> For fully fifteen minutes after I had taken the shoes off, my feet hurt me far worse than ever. Brother sat down and rubbed them, but that gave me no relief. Indeed, the pain was so great it made me sick at my stomach. But in half an hour I had the seams rubbed out of the hollows of my feet, so that they were back to their natural state again. But in that time I had made a firm determination never again to try to wear ready-made, narrow shoes. And that is one resolution I have carried out.

His extremely casual work clothes created an impression that Jack enjoyed immensely: Visitors would think he was simply a hired hand and not the noted naturalist himself. Manly is exceedingly fond of a story involving one particularly well-dressed gentleman. Apparently Jack had been leading the man on to believe he was one of the hired hands, and before he was able to reveal his true identity, the man abruptly cut him off. After asking Jack if this was all Mr. Miner kept him around to do, to which Jack replied in the affirmative, the man said, "Here's a quarter, go buy yourself a cigar."

Jack was most comfortable around the sanctuary when he was "dressed down."
(Miner Collection)

Jack Miner was also a committed family man who loved his wife deeply and worshipped his surviving children. He never totally recovered from the losses of Pearl and Carl and his much-missed brother Ted. In fact, at one point when talking about all the times he had stood at the graveside, Jack asserted, "Right down in my heart, had it been in my power, I would gladly have exchanged places with my loved one that he might rise up and be what I might have been." Jack also regularly proclaimed his devotion to his mother, and often referred to his respect for his father's opinions which he sought whenever matters weighed too heavily on his mind.

Being such a family- and home-oriented individual, he found the long absences his lecture tours required particularly hard, but he was so committed to raising the necessary funds to keep the geese fed and to spreading the idea of conservation across the land that he kept up these trips for thirty years. But it never became any easier. Manly remembers how pleased Jack always was to be back home: "He was just overjoyed . . . he was in a thankful mood, and he says, 'Why it's wonderful. I met Mr. and Mrs. So-and-So in this town and that town,' but he was more or less concerned about and happy to be home to see if the birds were all right."

While Jack was basically a simple God-loving person, there were some features of his character that were not so noble or admirable. But these flaws served to give his personality a fullness that prevented him from being reduced to the two-dimensionality of a cartoon character. One observer, for example, a local minister who got to know Jack in the late 1930s and felt he was essentially a sincere and well-intentioned person, wrote about Jack's great self-centredness: " 'I' is one of his great words. He is a profound egoist." In addition, the minister had the impression that Jack enjoyed the sound of his own voice as "he will monopolize ninety-nine and two-fifths of the conversation"—and in a somewhat odd observation, given his own profession, remarked, "Very likely in doing so he will preach you a sermon."

Jack's writings sometimes give a similar impression of a certain vanity and false modesty. In one passage, for example, he reels off a long list of his accomplishments but observes that he does not want to be boastful, for being boastful is a sin. Similarly, in his introduction to *Wild Goose Jack: Jack Miner, His Life and Religion*, he spends a page and a half outlining the various tributes he has received over the years in an attempt to explain why such an unlearned person should venture his views on religion and why anyone should bother reading them. And when he queries and answers himself as follows during this discussion, one gets the distinct impression of someone protesting too much: "Why am I not vain of such as honors . . . as these? Why? Because the tears of thankfulness to Almighty God, for His preserving care, and guidance and wisdom, blot out all selfish thoughts."

Even more troubling to a modern sensibility, however, is the presence of racial and ethnic stereotypes that suggest a certain ethnocentrisim or bigotry. At times Jack told "Ikie and Jakie" stories mimicking a Yiddish accent, and at one point described the Jew who used to buy the skunk pelts Jack trapped as a youngster, as having "an eye for business, as men of his race usually do." North American Indians were often characterized as "Injun Joe," and Jack would also recite their sayings in his impression of their dialect, as when he offered the following: "Everybody think like me, everybody want my squaw." Blacks, although not mentioned as frequently, were treated in a similar manner. Two black men visited the Kingsville area and held a revival camp, "convert[ing] all our darkies to the extreme bottom of their pockets." They also offered a lecture that Jack and Laona attended on the topic of the animals and birds of Central Africa. Jack described the one man as "smiling just enough to cause his teeth to gleam like African ivory," while the "face of the other glistened like a tar roof in the distance." Even the economical Scotsman received such treatment. "Sandy" was said to climb the fence gate to save the hinges, and it was his behaviour that gave bears a bad name for harassing tourists in recreational parks: "Yes, a bear did strike a man in Yellowstone Park, but it was a Scotsman who gave the wild bear a candy and then wanted to take it away from him, but bruin wouldn't stand for it and knocked Sandy over the log and that is all there was to it, but bruin went on eating the candy."

Jack's attitudes toward minorities were in keeping with the prevailing attitudes of the times, but are most unenlightened by modern-day standards. He was also extremely conservative about liquor, cigarettes, and amusements, even by the norms of the 1920s and 1930s. His strong words against drinking, smoking, and card-playing make him appear quite prudish. But Jack's dislike of "King Alcohol" is understandable; his father had a drinking problem that was so great that at one point, Jack contends, he moved the family to Canada to escape the tyranny of the drinking halls of Ohio. He decried Canada's activities during the Prohibition era in the United States, and characterized alcohol as ". . . this cursed beast. It is worse than a beast. It is a tempting, contagious cancer to the very best and biggest-hearted men."

As for smoking, Jack believed that 50 percent of all brush fires were caused by the careless discarding of cigarettes. The activity also contributed to many deaths through house, apartment, and hotel fires. Jack would tell how he and Ted "were disgusted and poisoned against liquor and tobacco," and how their abstinence had led to their steady nerves and accurate shots as hunters, and kept them out of trouble at dances. And as for playing cards, it was "a doubtful amusement" according to brother Ted. Jack always asserted, "I don't play cards, they often start quarrels." Besides, it wasted time that could be better spent being of "service to God and humanity."

In the larger scheme of things, especially when Jack's accomplishments in and contributions to the realm of conservation are considered, such shortcomings are relatively negligible flaws in a warmhearted public-spirited human being. The large-scale campaign he carried out to change public opinions and attitudes about wildlife and natural resources, and man's relationship to them, was immensely successful. As a child and young adult, John Jasperson was quite close to Jack and describes the approach he saw him utilize:

> He was the preacher. . . . He was the guy in charge—there
> was no question about that. He was a very impressive individual

in a crowd. . . . He was a salesman, he was a huckster . . . by any means possible he was going to persuade the rest of the world that Jack Miner's view was *the view* on the birds and the animals—and it was a great contribution to make too.

Jasper Miner feels that his father's source of inspiration to carry on such a campaign came from his belief that God had intended him to do so: "He was inspired, I think, that this was a place he was allotted in life . . . I think that is the greatest goal—if anyone can determine it—to find a place in life where they could feel a sense of accomplishment. And that's what he was feeling, a sense of accomplishing something and helping to improve nature . . ."

In addition to being a dedicated, pragmatic campaigner to save the world's wildlife, Jack is also pictured as a brilliant, often moody, visionary thinker. John Jasperson felt that the great men of the times were attracted to Jack and the sanctuary because they recognized in him a kindred spirit, a person who was not fettered by theories or concepts, but rather could see what was in front of him and respond to it as was necessary and appropriate. Jasperson characterized Jack as an artist and a dreamer:

> I felt as a man he was capable of great internal imagery. I look back as a more mature person who feels he knows something more about these things now, and I think, well, he was an artist really as a person—an artist is a person who can put things together . . . I think he was great for having a capacity to internalize his picture of what he thought should be there, and then go and implement that picture. He must have been a very visual man. I never asked him, but I think he must have been a dreamer.

Others who also knew him intimately report that, although Jack was usually outgoing and loved to talk and socialize, he regularly lapsed into periods of introspection and intense thought. At those times he seemed to be preoccupied, and it was obvious that he wanted to be left alone with his musings.

It was in the woods, as he communed with nature, that he became most completely involved and absorbed in such thought. For Jack there was nothing as invigorating, while at the same time soothing, as being surrounded by the so-called wild creatures out of doors:

> You go to the Zoo, to see birds and animals fighting the wire to get out—that is the usual condition in which you see them—and you hardly see what they look like. But to be hidden away, quietly, in their natural home and environment, gives one the privilege of seeing and knowing them as they really are, before man has any control over them. Yes, we pay fifty cents and upwards for a seat in a man-made Opera House to see and listen to a second-hand, artificial entertainment, but for mine, give me just ten minutes in any one of my many, many private seats in Nature's Cathedrals of this County, fifty years ago.

Almost to the end of his days, Jack spent time each fall "under canvas" in the solitude of the northern woods, far from civilization (ca. 1928). (Dr. R.D. Sloane)

Jack at his tent in his northern campsite (ca. 1931). (Dr. R.D. Sloane)

During one such sojourn in the woods, Jack formulated a prayer to God that came to be known as "Jack Miner's Testimony":

> One day as I sat in one of these Cathedrals of Nature, Heaven seemed to descend all about me, and as my mind's eyes flashed over my life I could see the barefoot, red-headed, freckle-faced, destitute pollywog-catcher, with just enough clothes to dust a fiddle. Him? Why he has no more chance in this world than a snowball in the oven! Then all in the same breath, my living-room fills to overflowing with gratitude, and my head sinks between my hands, and I wonder if great big David could possibly have more to be thankful for than I have. No, he could not. For I have *all* to be thankful for. He could not have had more. Then, as I started to repeat his twenty-third Psalm, David's prayer, it came to me in different words:

> "The Lord is my guide and teacher;
> I will not get lost.
> He makes my heart a receiving-station for His wireless.
> He sits down beside me in the pathless woods and opens up His book of knowledge; he [*sic*] turns the leaves very slowly, that my dimmed eyes may read His meaning.
> He makes the trees I plant grow, and flowers to arch my path with their fragrant beauty; He gives me dominion over the fowls of the air, and they honk and sing their way to and from my home.
> Yea, He has brought me up from a barefoot, underprivileged boy to be a man respected by millions of people,
> And I will give Him all the credit and praise, whenever, wherever, and forever."

Jack watches a train (his only link to civilization) approaching the vicinity of his northern campground (ca. 1928).
(Dr. R.D. Sloane)

Although more often than not Jack would couch his reaction to such experiences in the woods in Christian terms, there is a strong suggestion of a more universal spiritual or mystical element reminiscent of the transcendentalists, such as Emerson and Thoreau, for whom nature was beyond the grasp of human understanding and had to be experienced directly to be appreciated.

At about the same time that Jack started to write his memoirs at the beginning of the 1930s, Manly began to be concerned about the future of the sanctuary. The Great Depression had forced the Miners to put the brick and tile yard into receivership, and while Jack was still healthy and active and eager to continue his speaking tours, he was over sixty-five years old and, as he would say, "I'm getting a year older every twelve months." Manly realized that his father could not keep up the pace for much longer and that no one could really replace his magnetism and charisma, which drew the people to the lectures and fired their imagination. With the loss of income from the family business, the cessation of government grants, and the slackening of demand for speaking engagements during such hard economic times, clearly another source of financing had to

be secured to ensure the continued existence of the sanctuary.

Manly drew on his experience managing and promoting Jack's activities and on his considerable business acumen to come up with a solution.

> In 1931, looking ahead, I knew father couldn't be with us forever and while I didn't even have a public school education I educated myself along the lines I was most interested in and I read how great institutions like the New York Museum of Natural History, The New York Art Centre—The Smithsonian Institute—were all endowed by philanthropic-minded people . . .
>
> . . . my reasoning was if I had a sound legal set-up in the form of a Foundation or Trust, I was sure the people of America could be educated to give their money to perpetuate a Sanctuary where there are living birds as well as they perpetuate a museum [such as the Museum of Natural History] where they had dead birds and stuffed specimens.

Manly was named as heir to the sanctuary in Jack's will, but he considered it a "white elephant." He could have easily sold it to a millionaire as an estate, but "that would mean the place would pass out of existence as far as a public bird Sanctuary for birds and people was concerned."

To circumvent this possibility, Manly enlisted the aid of Detroit lawyer Henry M. Wallace to incorporate the Jack Miner Migratory Bird Foundation in the United States in 1931. In 1936 a Canadian foundation of the same name was incorporated by a special act of the Ontario Parliament. This meant that both United States and Canadian citizens could donate or bequeath funds to this foundation on a tax-exempt basis. In addition, the sanctuary property was deeded to the foundation; thus it could never be sold or mortgaged.

With a structure established to ensure the continuance of the sanctuary, the transition after Jack's death in 1944 was relatively smooth and uneventful. Manly continued to manage the business affairs of the sanctuary and devoted time and attention to raising financial support for the foundation, while Jasper took over the full operational routine of the sanctuary itself—which, of course, he had helped his father with when Jack was alive. This involved feeding and banding the geese and hosting the visitors who came each spring and fall.

After Jack's death the public profile of the sanctuary was not as high as when he was alive, but people remembered him and what he had accomplished, and they still visited the Miner home in large numbers during the migratory seasons. Between 5,000 and 10,000 cars a day would arrive during the peak period, and many thousands of schoolchildren and senior citizens would be bussed to the sanctuary during the course of a year. Manly and Jasper still hosted the rich, the famous, and the powerful: Cyrus Eaton, Norman Vincent Peale, Canadian Prime Minister John Diefenbaker, Ontario Premier Leslie Frost, officials from thirty-three delegations at the United

Opposite: Releasing geese became a ritual that Jack and his visitors enjoyed greatly. The Miners usually kept some geese in a special pen for just such occasions. (Dr. R.D. Sloane)

Overleaf: Over the years Jack and hundreds of thousands of visitors were photographed at the sanctuary grounds. People would often mail copies of their snapshots back to Jack. (Miner Collection)

Nations, and so on. All in all, it remained the second most popular tourist attraction in Ontario—surpassed only by Niagara Falls.

But Jack's sons also experienced some of the opposition and frustration that their father had. Shortly after Jack's death, for example, a wildlife bureaucrat from Ottawa was sent to the sanctuary to inform the Miners that in the future they would have to abandon the use of their Scripture-laden bands in favour of ones containing more scientific information. In Manly's words, this was "an action that hurt every one of us as a family and so deeply affected my younger brother [Jasper] that, though he [was] a man nearing fifty years of age, he wept." Fortunately for the Miners, Manly's intervention with the political leaders of the time prevented such a change, with the result that "all birds banded at the Jack Miner Sanctuary are still carrying the original Jack Miner band, and will do so as long as we band waterfowl here at the Sanctuary."

Jack Miner has never left his sanctuary. His body and that of Laona's are entombed on the sanctuary grounds in a sarcophagus that is often surrounded by Canada geese that they both loved so dearly. In life as well, Jack had the unique ability to mingle with these apprehensive birds without frightening them. As family friend Colonel Fred Jasperson recalls: "He could go out all by himself . . . and he would wander through with the geese and they wouldn't even be disturbed by him. I've actually seen that happen. . . . he'd just move around and the geese would almost be pals with him. It was definitely something that was uniquely Jack."

Moreover, the spirit of Jack Miner seems to linger still around the sanctuary grounds. Colonel Jasperson is one of the people who has expressed this kind of sentiment: "I felt that Jack was very close to, let us say, the things that were nothing more than a shadow of spirit up in the sky. It just seemed to pass off with me that this is the spirit of Jack that is very evident when it's all quiet [at the sanctuary] and there's nothing except the stars or the moon, with the odd time perhaps a goose or two would say something, and I felt that old Jack was listening to it all."

Jack Miner's spirit also lives on in the hearts and minds of Canadians since each year in April National Wildlife Week is observed in Canada in his memory. In 1947 the Canadian Parliament, in a rare demonstration of unanimity, passed a bill decreeing that each year the week in which the anniversary of Jack's birth falls (April 10) shall be designated National Wildlife Week. During the parliamentary debate, all political parties in the House of Commons had kind words for Jack's efforts, and the explanatory note to the bill described him as "the man who did more than any other to create public interest in the value of Canadian wildlife resources and consideration for their natural habitats." And thirty years later, Manly and

JACK MINER

The
**Jack Miner Migratory Bird
Foundation, Inc.**

❖

"Letter Creating the Trust Estate"
"Articles of Association"
"Trustee Agreement"

Front cover of the documents incorporating the foundation in the United States in 1931 to ensure the continued existence of the sanctuary.
(Miner Collection)

Jasper Miner were also honoured when the University of Windsor conferred on them Honourary Doctor of Laws degrees. The citation from this occasion reads in part:

> Working as a team with a sensible division of labour these two men have not merely kept the original institution of their father in being, but have strengthened and expanded it. . . . All this represents an arduous and unselfish effort over sixty years, from the time when they were small boys helping their father. From an early age they fastened upon a fundamental principal [*sic*] of practical idealism, and all Canadians must be proud of their accomplishment.

The Jack Miner Migratory Bird Sanctuary exists today as a concrete manifestation of such "practical idealism." It is a tangible legacy that Jack Miner and his sons leave to the world. It is a reminder that someone who lives a life of destruction and slaughter can transform himself into a protector of wildlife and a promoter of the cause of conservation. It is a ray of light in a world in which man and nature are threatened with darkness.

The last photo taken of Jack Miner and his three sons (from left) Jasper, Manly, and Ted, in 1942.
(Don McCoy)

Appendix
Extinct Vertebrate Species in Taxonomic Order*

Species	Habitat Location	Approximate Date of Extinction
FISHES		
Blackfin Cisco	Lakes Michigan and Huron, USA and Canada	1960
Deepwater Cisco	Lakes Michigan and Huron, USA and Canada	1960
New Zealand Grayling†	New Zealand	1923
Thicktail Chub	California	1854
Stumptooth Minnow	Chihuahua, Mexico	1930
Parras Roundnose Minnow	Chihuahua, Mexico	1930
Big Spring Spinedace	Nevada	1950
Pahranagat Spinedace	Nevada	1950
Grass Valley Speckled Dace	Nevada	1950
Harelip Sucker	Central USA	1893
Shortnose Sucker	Oregon	1960
June Sucker	Utah	1959
Spring Valley Sucker	Nevada	1950
Lake Titicaca Orestias	Peru-Bolivia Border	1950
Parras Pupfish	Chihuahua, Mexico	1930
Ash Meadows Killifish	Nevada	1948
Tecopa Pupfish†	California	1960
Pahrump Killifish	Nevada	1950
Utah Lake Sculpin	Utah	1936
AMPHIBIANS		
Palestine Painted Frog	Hula Lake, Israel-Syria Border	1956
Vegas Valley Leopard Frog	Nevada	1966
REPTILES		
Rodriguez Greater Tortoise	Rodriguez and satellites	1800
Rodriguez Lesser Tortoise	Rodriguez and satellites	1800
Mauritian Domed Tortoise	Mauritius and satellites	1700
Mauritian High-Fronted Tortoise	Mauritius and satellites	1700
Réunion Tortoise (indica)	Réunion	1760
Réunion Tortoise (borbonica)	Réunion	1773
Marion's (Seychelles) Tortoise	Seychelles and Amirante Islands	1918

*Derived from David Day, *The Doomsday Book of Animals: A Natural History of Vanished Species* (Rexdale, Ontario: John Wiley & Sons Canada Limited, 1981).

†Rumours of survival

Species	Habitat Location	Approximate Date of Extinction
Barrington Island Tortoise	Galapagos Islands	1890
Charles Island Tortoise	Galapagos Islands	1876
Abingdon Island Tortoise	Galapagos Islands	1957
Narborough Island Tortoise	Galapagos Islands	1906
Rodriguez Day Gecko	Rodriguez and satellites	1920
Rodriguez Night Gecko	Rodriguez and satellites	1841
Jamaican Iguana	West Indies	1968
Navassa Iguana	West Indies	1966
Navassa Island Lizard	West Indies	1900
Martinique Lizard	West Indies	1837
Martinique Giant Ameiva	West Indies	1960
Grand Islet (Guadeloupe) Ameiva	West Indies	1920
Jamaican Giant Galliwasp	West Indies	1880
Ratas Island Lizard	Ratas Island Minorca	1950
San Stephano Lizard	San Stephano Island, Tyrrhenia Sea	1965
Mauritian Giant Skink	Mauritius	1650
Réunion Skink	Réunion	1880
Cape Verde Giant Skink	Cape Verde Islands, East Atlantic	1940
Round Island Boa	Round Island, Mauritius	1980
Jamaica Tree Snake	West Indies	1960
St. Croix Tree Snake	West Indies	1950
Martinique Racer	West Indies	1962
St. Lucia Racer	West Indies	1973
BIRDS		
Arabian Ostrich†	Syria and Arabia	1941
Tasmanian Emu	Tasmania	1850
Dwarf Emu	Kangaroo Island	1830
Moas	New Zealand	1500-1850
Elephant Bird	Madagascar	1700
Guadalupe Storm Petrel	Guadalupe, Mexican Pacific	1911
Stellar's Spectacled Cormorant	Bering Island and satellites, Bering Sea	1850
Bonin Night Heron	Bonin Islands, Northwest Pacific	1879
Coues' Gadwall	Washington Island, Central Pacific	1874
Korean Crested Shelduck	Korea and Japan	1916
Pink-headed Duck	Upper Bengal, India	1942
Labrador Duck	New England and Canadian Maritime Provinces	1875
Auckland Island Merganser	Auckland Island, New Zealand	1910
Painted Vulture	Florida, USA	1800
Madagascar Serpent Eagle†	Northeast Madagascar	1950
Guadalupe Caracara (Quelili)	Guadalupe, Mexican Pacific	1900

†Rumours of survival

Species	Habitat Location	Approximate Date of Extinction
Heath Hen	New England States, USA	1932
New Zealand Quail	New Zealand	1868
Himalayan Mountain Quail	Eastern Punjab, India	1870
Wake Island Rail	Wake Island, North Pacific	1945
Tahiti Rail	Society Islands	1900
Modest Rail	Chatham Islands, New Zealand	1900
Dieffenbach's Rail	Chatham Islands, New Zealand	1840
Macquarie Island Banded Rail	Macquarie Island, New Zealand, Southern Ocean	1880
Jamaican Wood Rail (or Uniform Rail)	Jamaica	1881
Mauritian Red Rail	Mauritius	1680
Leguat's Rail	Rodriguez	1700
Laysan Rail (or Spotless Crake)	Laysan, Hawaii	1944
Sandwich Rail	Hawaii	1884
Kittlitz's Rail	Kusoie and Ponape, Caroline Islands, North Pacific	1850
Little St. Helena Rail	St. Helena	1680
Fiji Barred-Winged Rail†	Fiji Islands	1965
Iwo Jima Rail	Iwo Jima, North Pacific	1924
White Gallinule	Lord Howe Island, Tasman Sea	1830
Samoan Wood Rail	Savaii, Samoa, Central Pacific	1873
Tristan Gallinule (or Island Hen)	Tristan da Cunha, South Atlantic	1890
Eskimo Curlew†	North and South America	1970
Tahitian Sandpiper	Tahiti	1800
Moorean Sandpiper	Moorea, Society Islands	1800
Jerdon's Doublebanded Courser	Eastern Ghats, India	1900
Great Auk	North Atlantic Islands	1844
Dodo	Mauritius	1680
Rodriguez Solitaire	Rodriguez	1780
Réunion Solitaire	Réunion	1700
White Dodo	Réunion	1770
Bonin Wood Pigeon	Bonin Islands, Northwest Pacific	1900
Lord Howe Island Pigeon	Lord Howe Island, Tasman Sea	1853
Passenger Pigeon	Eastern North America	1914
Tanna Dove	Tanna, New Hebrides, West Pacific	1800
Choiseul Crested Pigeon	Choiseul, Solomon Islands, West Pacific	1910
Pigeon Hollandaise	Mauritius	1826

†Rumours of survival

Species	Habitat Location	Approximate Date of Extinction
Norfolk Island Pigeon	Norfolk Island, New Zealand	1801
Norfolk Island Kaka	Norfolk and Phillip Islands, New Zealand	1851
New Caledonian Lorikeet†	New Caledonia, Southwest Pacific	1860
Yellow-headed Macaw	Jamaica	1765
Green and Yellow Macaw	Jamaica	1842
Dominican Macaw	Dominica, West Indies	1800
Cuban Red Macaw	Cuba	1864
Labat's Conure	Guadeloupe, West Indies	1722
Puerto Rican Conure	Mona Island, Puerto Rico	1892
Western Carolina Parakeet	Louisiana, USA	1910
Eastern Carolina Parakeet	Carolina and Virginia, USA	1914
Guadeloupe Amazon	Guadeloupe, West Indies	1750
Martinique Amazon	Martinique, West Indies	1750
Culebra Island Amazon	Culebra Island, Puerto Rico	1899
Broad-billed Parrot	Mauritius	1650
Rodriguez Parrot	Rodriguez	1800
Mascarene Parrot	Réunion	1840
Seychelles Parakeet	Seychelles	1881
Réunion Ring-necked Parakeet	Réunion	1800
Rodriguez Ring-necked Parakeet	Rodriguez	1880
Black-fronted Parakeet	Tahiti	1850
Macquarie Island Parakeet	New Zealand, Southern Ocean	1890
Red-fronted Parakeet	Lord Howe Island, Tasman Sea	1869
Delalande's Madagascar Coucal	Madagascar	1920
Mauritian Barn Owl	Mauritius	1700
Newton's Barn Owl	Mauritius	1700
Comoro Scops Owl	Anjouan, Comoro Islands, Indian Ocean	1890
Commerson's Scops Owl	Mauritius	1850
South Island Laughing Owl†	South Island, New Zealand	1900
North Island Laughing Owl	North Island, New Zealand	1900
Forest Spotted Owlet	Central India	1914
Rodriguez Little Owl	Rodriguez	1850
Antigua Burrowing Owl	Antigua, Nevis and St. Kitts, West Indies	1900
Guadeloupe Burrowing Owl	Marie Galante, West Indies	1900
Jamaican Pauraqué	Jamaica	1859
Ryukyu (Miyako) Kingfisher	Ryukyu Islands, Japan	1887
American Ivory-billed Woodpecker†	Southeast USA	1972

†Rumours of survival

Species	Habitat Location	Approximate Date of Extinction
Guadalupe Flicker	Guadalupe, Mexican Pacific	1906
Stephen Island Wren	Stephen Island, New Zealand	1894
North Island Bush Wren	North Island, New Zealand	1900
Stead's Bush Wren	Stewart Island and satellites, New Zealand	1965
Guadalupe Bewick's Wren	Guadalupe, Mexican Pacific	1892
Martinique House Wren	Martinique	1900
St. Lucia House Wren	St. Lucia	1971
Bonin Island Thrush (Grosbeak)	Peel Island, Bonin Group North Pacific	1828
Bay Thrush	Raiatea, Society Islands	1780
Lanai Omao	Lanai, Hawaii	1931
Oahu Omao	Oahu, Hawaii	1825
Molokai Omao	Molokai, Hawaii	1936
Lord Howe Island Vinous-tinted Blackbird	Lord Howe Island, Tasman Sea	1920
Chatham Island Fernbird	Chatham Island, New Zealand	1895
Laysan Millerbird	Laysan, Hawaii	1920
Lord Howe Island Flycatcher	Lord Howe Island	1920
Tonga Tabu Tahiti Flycatcher	Tonga Tabu (Tongatupu), Central Pacific	1800
Lord Howe Island Fantail	Lord Howe Island	1924
Lord Howe Island White Eye	Lord Howe Island	1923
Marianne Seychelles White Eye	Seychelles	not given
Kioea	Island of Hawaii	1850
Hawaiian O-O	Island of Hawaii	1934
Oahu O-O	Oahu, Hawaii	1837
Molokai O-O	Molokai, Hawaii	1904
Chatham Island Bellbird	Chatham Islands, New Zealand	1906
St. Kitts Puerto Rican Bullfinch	Puerto Rico	1900
Clouded Galapagos Finch	Galapagos Islands	not given
Guadalupe Rufous-sided Towhee	Guadalupe Island, Mexican Pacific	1900
Great Amakihi	Hawaii	1900
Molokai Alauwahio	Molokai, Hawaii	1970
Lanai Alauwahio	Lanai, Hawaii	1937
Oahu Akepa	Oahu, Hawaii	1900
Hawaiian Akioloa	Island of Hawaii	1940
Lanai Akioloa	Lanai, Hawaii	1894
Oahu Akioloa	Oahu, Hawaii	1840
Kauai Akioloa	Kauai, Hawaii	1965
Oahu Nukupuu	Oahu, Hawaii	1890
Kauai Nukupuu	Kauai, Hawaii	1965
Maui Nukupuu	Maui, Hawaii	1896

Species	Habitat Location	Approximate Date of Extinction
Greater Koa Finch	Hawaii	1896
Lesser Koa Finch	Hawaii	1891
Koa Finch	Hawaii	1894
Laysan Apapane	Laysan	1925
Ula-Ai-Hawane	Hawaii	1892
Mamo	Hawaii	1898
Black Mamo	Molokai, Hawaii	1907
São Thomé Grosbeak	São Thomé Island, Gulf of Guinea	1900
Réunion Fody	Réunion	1776
Kusaie Mountain Starling	Kusaie, Caroline Islands, Southwest Pacific	1827
Mysterious Starling	Society Islands	1780
Lord Howe Island Starling	Lord Howe Island, Tasman Sea	1925
Bourbon (Réunion) Crested Starling	Réunion	1868
White Mascarene Starling	Rodriguez	1840
Rodriguez (Slater's) Starling	Rodriguez	not given
Huia†	North Island, New Zealand	1907
MAMMALS		
Toolache Wallaby	South Australia	1940
Eastern Hare-Wallaby	Southeastern Australia	1890
Gilbert's Potoroo	Western Australia	1900
Broad-faced Potoroo	Western Australia	1908
St. Francis Island Potoroo	St. Francis Island, Great Australian Bight	1900
Eastern Barred Bandicoot	New South Wales and Victoria	1940
Western Barred Bandicoot	Western Australia	1910
Pig-footed Bandicoot	South Australia	1907
Greater Rabbit-Bandicoot	South Australia	1930
Thylacine (or Tasmanian Wolf)†	Tasmania	1933
Christmas Island Musk Shrew	Christmas Island, Indian Ocean	1900
Puerto Rican Nesophont	West Indies	1650
Cuban Nesophont	West Indies	1650
Cuban Long-nosed Nesophont	West Indies	1650
Hispaniolan Nesophont	West Indies	1930
Lesser Hispaniolan Nesophont	West Indies	1930
Least Hispaniolan Nesophont	West Indies	1930
Jamaican Long-tailed Bat	Jamaica	1900
Puerto Rican Long-tongued Bat	Puerto Rico	1850
Haitian Long-tongued Bat	Hispaniola	1900

†Rumours of survival

Species	Habitat Location	Approximate Date of Extinction
Lesser Falcate-winged Bat	Cuba	1750
Puerto Rican Long-nosed Bat	Puerto Rico	1850
Cuban Yellow Bat	Cuba	1850
Captain Maclear's Rat	Christmas Island, Indian Ocean	1900
Bulldog Rat	Christmas Island, Indian Ocean	1900
South Australia Spiny-haired Rat	Kangaroo Island	1850
Cuban Short-tailed Hutia	Cuba	1850
Crooked Island Hutia	Crooked Island	1600
Great Abaco Hutia	Great Abaco	1600
Hispaniolan Hexolobodon	Hispaniola	1600
Hispaniolan Hutia	Hispaniola	1750
Puerto Rican Isolobodon	Puerto Rico	1700
Haitian (Hispaniolan) Isolobodon	Hispaniola	1550
Hispaniolan Narrow-toothed Hutia	Hispaniola	1600
Hispaniolan Spiny Rat	Hispaniola	1600
Lesser Hispaniolan Spiny Rat	Hispaniola	1600
Cuban Spiny Rat	Cuba	1870
Lesser Cuban Spiny Rat	Cuba	1870
Puerto Rican 'Agouti'	Puerto Rico	1750
Lesser Puerto Rican 'Agouti'	Puerto Rico	1750
Jamaican Rice Rat	Jamaica	1880
St. Vincent Rice Rat	St. Vincent, West Indies	1900
Martinique Musk Rat	West Indies	1900
St. Lucia Musk Rat	West Indies	1880
Barbuda Musk Rat	West Indies	1600
Puerto Rican Quemi	Puerto Rico	1500
Haitian Quemi	Haiti	1700
Puerto Rican Caviomorph	Puerto Rico	1600
Newfoundland White Wolf	Newfoundland, Canada	1911
Kenai Wolf	Kenai Peninsula, Alaska	1915
Texas Grey Wolf	Western Texas to Northeastern Mexico	1920
New Mexican Wolf	Central Arizona and New Mexico	1920
Great Plains Lobo Wolf	Southern Manitoba and Saskatchewan, southward to Texas	1926
Southern Rocky Mountain Wolf	Nevada, Utah and Colorado	1940
Cascade Mountains Brown Wolf	British Columbia south to Washington State	1950
Northern Rocky Mountain Wolf	not given	not given
Florida Black Wolf	Southeastern USA	1917
Texas Red Wolf	Texas	1970
Shamanu (or Japanese Wolf)	Japan	1905

Species	Habitat Location	Approximate Date of Extinction
Warrah (or Antarctic Wolf)	Falkland Islands	1876
Atlas Bear	North Africa	1870
Mexican Silver Grizzly	Northern Mexico	1964
Kamchatkan Bear	Kamchatkan Peninsula, USSR	1920
Sea Mink	New England	1880
Barbary Lion	North Africa	1922
Cape Lion	Cape Colony, South Africa	1865
Bali Tiger	Bali, Indonesia	1937
Arizona Jaguar	Southwestern USA	1905
Caribbean Monk Seal	Caribbean Sea	1952
Steller's Sea Cow†	Bering Sea	1767
Tarpan	Eastern Europe and Western Asia	1887
Syrian Onager	Middle East	1930
Quagga	South Africa	1883
Burchell's Zebra	South Africa	1910
Schomburgk's Deer	Eastern Siam (Thailand)	1932
Eastern Elk (Wapiti)	Eastern United States and Canada	1877
Merriam's Elk (Wapiti)	New Mexico and Arizona, USA	1906
Dawson's Caribou†	Queen Charlotte Islands, British Columbia, Canada	1908
Greenland Tundra Reindeer	Eastern Greenland	1950
Aurochs	Europe	1627
Caucasian Wisent	Caucasian Russia	1925
Eastern Buffalo (Bison)	Eastern USA	1825
Oregon Buffalo (Bison)	Oregon, Idaho and California, USA	1850
Blue Buck	Zwellendam, Cape Colony, South Africa	1799
Bubal Hartebeest	Algerian desert and Moroccan High Atlas	1923
Cape Red Hartebeest	South Africa	1940
Rufous Gazelle	Algeria	1940
Portuguese Ibex	Galicia and Northwest Iberian Mountains	1892
Pyrenean Ibex	French and Spanish Pyrenees	1910
Badlands (Audubon's) Bighorn Sheep	Dakotas and Nebraska, USA	1925

†Rumours of survival

Bibliography

Adams, Alexander B. *Eleventh Hour: A Hard Look at Conservation and the Future*. New York: G.P. Putnam's Sons, 1970.

Bodsworth, Fred. "Billy Sunday of the Birds." *Maclean*'s, May 11, 1952.

Brooks, Paul. *Speaking for Nature: How Literary Naturalists from Henry Thoreau to Rachel Carson Have Shaped America*. Boston: Houghton Mifflin Company, 1980.

Canadian Wildlife Administration. Ottawa: Canadian Wildlife Service, Environment Canada, 1982.

Clepper, Henry. *Leaders of American Conservation*. New York: The Ronald Press Company, 1971.

Day, David. *The Doomsday Book of Animals: A Natural History of Vanished Species*. Toronto: John Wiley & Sons Canada Limited, 1981.

Dorst, Jean. *The Migration of Birds*. Boston: Houghton Mifflin Company, 1962.

Fitter, Richard. *Vanishing Wild Animals of the World*. London: Midland Book Ltd. in association with Kaye & Ward Ltd., 1968.

Foster, Janet. *Working for Wildlife: The Beginning of Preservation in Canada*. Toronto: University of Toronto Press, 1978.

Graham, Frank, Jr. *Man's Dominion: The Story of Conservation in America*. New York: M. Evans and Company, 1971.

Hochbaum, H. Albert. *Travels and Traditions of Waterfowl*. Newton, Massachusetts: Charles T. Branford Company, 1960.

Linduska, Joseph P. (ed.). *Waterfowl Tomorrow*. Washington, D.C.: The United States Department of the Interior, 1964.

Litteljohn, Bruce M., and Pimlott, Douglas H. (ed.) *Why Wilderness: A report on mismanagement in Lake Superior Provincial Park*. Toronto: new press, 1971.

Livingston, John A. *The Fallacy of Wildlife Conservation*. Toronto: McClelland and Stewart Limited, 1981.

McCann, Lester J. *A New Day for Wildlife: A Fresh Approach*. St. Paul, Minnesota: Ramaley Printing Co., 1978.

McCoy, J. J. *Wild Enemies*. New York: Hawthorn Books, Inc., 1974.

McHenry, Robert (ed.) (with Van Doren, Charles). *A Documentary History of Conservation in America*. New York: Praeger Publishers, 1972.

Miner, Jack. *Jack Miner and the Birds*. (Memorial Edition) Kingsville, Ontario: The Jack Miner Migratory Bird Foundation, n.d.

——— . *Wild Goose Jack: Jack Miner, His Life and Religion*. Kingsville, Ontario: The Jack Miner Migratory Bird Foundation, 1969.

Miner, Manly F. *Famous Men I Have Known*. Kingsville, Ontario: The Jack Miner Migratory Bird Foundation, n.d.

——— . *Jack Miner: His Advice, Suggestions and a few of his Accomplishments*. Kingsville, Ontario: The Jack Miner Migratory Bird Foundation, 1972.

——— . *My Father—Jack Miner: Jack Miner's Conservation Policy, His Philosophy and Reasoning*. Kingsville, Ontario: The Jack Miner Migratory Bird Foundation, n.d.

——— . "My Most Unforgettable Character—Jack Miner," *Reader's Digest*, May 1969.

——— . *Practical Ideas About Conservation and Predator Control*. Kingsville, Ontario: The Jack Miner Migratory Bird Foundation, n.d.

Mycio, Luba (ed.). *Wildlife Management*, Learning About Wildlife Series, Unit 1. Ottawa: Canadian Wildlife Federation, 1983.

Nelson, E. W. "Bird Banding, The Telltale of Migratory Flight: A Modern Method of Learning the Flight-Ways and Habits of Birds." Special Reprint from *The National Geographic* Magazine. Washington, D.C.: Press of Judd & Detweiler, Inc., 1927.

Petulla, Joseph M. *American Environmentalism: Values, Tactics, Priorities*. College Station, Texas: Texas A & M University Press, 1980.

Rain, David, Linton, James M., Moore, Calvin W., and Murphy, Michael D. *Wild Goose Jack* (film). Toronto: Clear Horizon Films, Inc., 1982.

Reiger, John F. *American Sportsmen and the Origins of Conservation*. New York: Winchester Press, 1975.

Simon, Noel, and Géroudet, Paul. *Last Survivors*. New York: World Publishing Company, 1970.

Trefethen, James B. *An American Crusade for Wildlife*. New York: Winchester Press, 1975.

Zurhorst, Charles. *The Conservation Fraud*. Toronto: General Publishing Company, Ltd., 1970.

Index

Picture Credits

The bulk of the black and white images in the book are from the Miner Collection, as graciously provided by the Jack Miner Migratory Bird Foundation. Almost all of those photographs were taken by Dr. R. D. Sloane, a Leamington, Ontario, dentist, who became Jack's personal photographer, and seems to have spent as much time behind the lens as he did behind the drill. Stills have also been taken from motion pictures made over almost a thirty-year period by Ed Flickenger, a Ford Motor Company cameraman. In addition, Robert Kennedy kindly provided what is possibly the only surviving image of Jack's brother, Ted; while the Roy Studio made available an impressive image of the effects in Peterborough of Jack's birdhouse-building campaign. Colin Farmer supplied a rare view of Jack with children at camps.

Helen Trotter used consummate skill and aesthetic sensibility to bring several faded and deteriorating photographs back to life, and Henry Yee did the same in reproducing images from original negatives and motion picture footage. General archival material was helpfully provided by the Glenbow Museum (with the useful intervention of Dave Seeler), the Denver Public Library—Western History Department, Masterfile, and The Image Bank of Canada. Most of the total collection of black and white materials were hunted down and organized by Cal Moore; some were found by Mike Murphy—who also, of course, used his skills as a professional photographer to record colour images that capture the feel of the contemporary Miner Sanctuary.